PSYCHEDELIC

CANNABIS

———

"Is a highly reliable botanical psychedelic legally available throughout most of the US? The answer is a resounding 'yes,' and the
details of that answer reside in this book. As with many discoveries in this field, it began with McQueen's serendipitous discovery
of how, with the proper dose, intention, set, and setting, marijuana
can produce the same psychedelic effects that occur with 'classical' compounds like DMT and psilocybin. This book provides
guidance every step of the way: personal preparation, selection of
cannabis strains, methods for 'getting enough,' managing the experience, and integration. Most highly recommended!"

RICK STRASSMAN, M.D., AUTHOR OF
DMT: THE SPIRIT MOLECULE

"Daniel McQueen, the founder of the Center for Medicinal
Mindfulness, is a pioneer in the therapeutic uses of cannabis as
a psychedelic. Although we don't usually think of the cannabis
plant as a transformational psychedelic, Daniel shares information
that shows it to be just as profound and therapeutically effective as
'classical' psychedelics, such as psilocybin. Readers will find much
wisdom and good information in this book."

DENNIS MCKENNA, PH.D., ETHNOPHARMACOLOGIST, FOUNDER
AND PRESIDENT OF MCKENNA ACADEMY, AND
COAUTHOR OF *THE INVISIBLE LANDSCAPE*

"Daniel and his much-needed Medicinal Mindfulness program use cannabis to heighten emotional and spiritual healing and awakening to provide an urgently needed user-support system. Cannabis nurtures honesty, insight, peace of mind, and emotional healing, and *Psychedelic Cannabis* provides expert professional guidance in encouraging these uplifting experiences while high."

JOHN SELBY, AUTHOR OF
CANNABIS FOR COUPLES

PSYCHEDELIC
CANNABIS

Therapeutic Methods and Unique Blends to Treat Trauma and Transform Consciousness

DANIEL McQUEEN

Park Street Press

Rochester, Vermont

Park Street Press
One Park Street
Rochester, Vermont 05767
www.ParkStPress.com

Text stock is SFI certified

Park Street Press is a division of Inner Traditions International

Cataloging-in-Publication Data for this title is available from the Library of Congress

ISBN 978-1-64411-338-7 (print)
ISBN 978-1-64411-339-4 (ebook)

Printed and bound in the United States by Lake Book Manufacturing, Inc. The text stock is SFI certified. The Sustainable Forestry Initiative® program promotes sustainable forest management.

10 9 8 7 6 5 4 3 2 1

Text design and layout by Virginia Scott Bowman
This book was typeset in Garamond Premier Pro with Majesty and Architecta used as the display typefaces

To send correspondence to the author of this book, mail a first-class letter to the author c/o Inner Traditions • Bear & Company, One Park Street, Rochester, VT 05767, and we will forward the communication, or contact the author directly at **medicinalmindfulness.org**.

For Alison

Note to the Reader

This book is intended as an informational guide and should not be a substitute for professional medical care or therapeutic treatment. Any application of the material set forth in the following pages is at the reader's discretion and is his or her sole responsibility. Neither the author nor the publisher can assume any responsibility for physical, psychological, legal, or social consequences resulting from the ingestion of cannabis and/or psychedelic substances or their derivatives. While the publisher and author have used their best efforts in preparing this book, they make no representations or warranties with respect to its accuracy or completeness. In addition, this book contains no legal or medical advice; please consult a licensed professional if appropriate.

Contents

PART THREE

PREPARING FOR THE PSYCHEDELIC CANNABIS EXPERIENCE

PART FOUR

THE CAPTAIN PROTOCOL

A Family of Practices for Using Psychedelic Cannabis for Healing

Foreword

Stephen Gray

You've noticed I'm sure that we live in extraordinary times of immense and rapid change, a period both exciting and dangerous—ominous even. Though nobody really knows how the plotline will unfold in the decades to come, there is one thing I feel confident in proclaiming: a widespread and radical consciousness transformation is urgently needed on this beleaguered blue planet if humanity is to come through this era in anything resembling sane and sustainable conditions.

With that principle in mind, the next "bold" proclamation is that those of us willing to embrace and meet the changes and challenges—you might call this amorphous congregation the (at least aspiring) spiritual warriors of love and intelligence—must be open to *all* available tools, alone and in syncretic combination, without dogmatic limitations and divisions.

There are a number of plants and semisynthetic and synthetic substances known as psychedelics or entheogens that are arguably *the* most potent tools available for these urgent times. In appropriate conditions these substances are capable of pulling back the curtain of illusion that has obscured an eternal and unconditioned reality beyond imagining. They can show us where we need to heal and to free ourselves from the bonds of our past, and they can invite us to see and be inspired by a normally cloud-covered but always present divine reality.

Many of us are now aware of the potential of what you might call the "major psychedelics." Ayahuasca, psilocybin mushrooms, peyote, LSD, and several others are in this category and are getting increasing attention almost weekly. But there is one humble plant that has until recently never received its due. For reasons not necessary to describe here, this plant has been outlawed, disdained, mocked, and ignored, especially in the past century or so but here and there throughout the long course of history as well.

We are now experiencing an exciting and promising renaissance of understanding and use of our ancient friend and ally, cannabis. But even the majority of those sympathetic to the pleasures and medical potential of the plant are still largely unaware of its remarkable capability as a healing and awakening sacramental medicine when used in optimal conditions.

Daniel McQueen is most definitely aware of this potential, and he has now added his authentic—and bold—voice to a still-small but growing brother-/sisterhood of compassionate visionaries intent on correcting this serious misapprehension and missed potential. As you read this book it will become clear very quickly that Daniel is thoroughly qualified for the mission. I've seen the power of cannabis for this essential healing and awakening work, but I'm not sure I've ever encountered anyone in "modern" society who has so effectively mastered and articulated the understanding and techniques necessary for people to discover and experience the full capability of the psychedelic (mind and soul manifesting) use of cannabis.

Daniel puts his cards right out on the table in the very first paragraph of the book to set the agenda for all that follows. He says that cannabis "might just be the most accessible and effective psychedelic medicine we have available for healing and transformational purposes." A bold claim indeed and certain to be controversial in some circles, but as I suggested above, he clearly has the cattle to go with that big hat.

Psychedelic Cannabis is a straightforward and accessible book with an unambiguous mission. In Daniel's words again: "I'd like to teach you exactly how to turn cannabis into a real psychedelic medicine and how to safely and effectively use it for healing and transformation." No muddled or mixed message there and now that I've read the book, I'm fully confident that he has accomplished that task extraordinarily well.

In as much as Daniel has a rare grasp of the depths of working with cannabis toward healing and awakening, he is also a skillful communicator and educator. The word *teach* in the above quote is right on the mark. Daniel speaks directly and intimately to the reader and his language is crystal clear. He comes through these pages like your favorite teacher, the one you remember who cares about his students and is determined to give them everything they need to step out into the world on their own. This is not a book of theory and speculation; it's an eminently practical guide that has been thoroughly tempered in the crucible of extensive experience. As Daniel says, he has "facilitated sessions for thousands of people in individual and group psychotherapy settings and journey experiences" with our ancient plant ally as the powerful yet kindly sacrament.

One of the reasons many of us are convinced that cannabis will play an increasingly important—even central—role in the human community in the years, decades, and centuries to come is its unassailable and permanent status as the "people's plant." A key component of the consciousness transformation revolution is the dawning realization that we are ultimately our own healers and that we are much more deeply interrelated and intertwined with the community of souls at multiple levels than almost all of us have realized. More and more of us are gradually learning to soften the self-protecting barriers we've built and discover the truth of our connectedness to "all our relations," as the Native Americans have often said it.

A major aspect of this radical reawakening is the understanding of our relationship to medicine. In perhaps the most important sense, nobody owns cannabis. The people's plant is one of the major medicine plants of this planet, in some respects perhaps *the* most widely applicable of all plants. I believe we in the so-called modern societies are in the early stages of a huge shift toward the recognition of the many healing plants, our relationship with them, and our responsibility for preserving and promoting them and the knowledge of their use.

I was happy to see that Daniel understands that principle—the spirit of cannabis you might say, one of "community, ecology, and sharing." Some of us like to occasionally joke that cannabis is indeed a gateway drug—a gateway to a reenvisioned and revitalized understanding of medicine, of healing, and of our relationship to plant and planet altogether.

Our ancient friend and ally is also a gateway or forerunner, opening pathways toward a renaissance of understanding and legal recognition of the more controversial psychedelic medicines such as psilocybin mushrooms, ayahuasca, and LSD. It's an exciting time in this field, and Daniel's wonderful book is doing more than its share to advance this necessary renaissance.

All that said, once I had read the full text, it was uncontestably clear that above all *Psychedelic Cannabis* is a masterful guidebook for all of us who would like to find out for ourselves through experience the full potential for healing and awakening that the skillful use of cannabis provides, healing ourselves first as a solid foundation and then extending our awakening hearts and vision outward.

This isn't a book you'll read once and consign to a bookshelf forever after. If you grasp its potential and decide to make use of it in your spiritual and healing work with cannabis, you will want to keep it close at hand. The book is overflowing with specific suggestions for all stages and aspects of the work, collected from Daniel's long experience. I envision dog-eared copies with bookmarks and highlighted text sitting in plain sight in living rooms and ceremonial spaces everywhere.

I've been around cannabis for over fifty years. I've taught principles and practices for working with cannabis as a spiritual ally, and I've been leading cannabis ceremonies for over ten years. I say this not to draw attention to myself but in the hope of asserting some street cred for proclaiming that you can count on this book. You can trust its thoroughly field-tested, compassionate guidance. If you apply that guidance to your work with cannabis, however that manifests, you *will* be on the right track.

There is great promise in these pages. So please read, absorb, and apply.

STEPHEN GRAY is a writer, editor, speaker, cannabis ceremony leader, and Spirit Plant Medicine Conference organizer. He is the author of *Returning to Sacred World: A Toolkit for the Emerging Reality* and editor of/contributor to *Cannabis and Spirituality: An Explorer's Guide to an Ancient Plant Spirit Ally*. Find him online at his website and Facebook page both titled Cannabis and Spirituality.

Hemp is a holy and essential plant.
Listen to the Hemp people.
The Hemp people will show you the way out of the
darkness we have made.
Be good to each other.
There is enough trouble in the world.

PEYOTE WAY CHURCH

Ace of Buds. Art by Eliot Alexander.

A Responsibility
and an Acknowledgment

I personally identify with openness and sharing and am inspired by collaborative efforts. The psychedelic movement has greatly benefited from open science practices, and in turn, open psychedelic practices have greatly benefited society. When the Statement on Open Science and Open Praxis with Psilocybin, MDMA, and Similar Substances was proposed in 2017 (page xx), my practice, the Center for Medicinal Mindfulness, became a signatory of it. I'm particularly inspired by the following part of the agreement, signed by leaders of the psychedelic research community:

> We will strive to make our expertise and services available to all who may benefit from them, even those whose means are limited. . . . We will not withhold, nor will we require others to withhold, materials or knowledge (experiences, observations, discoveries, methods, best practices, or the like) for commercial advantage. . . . We will strive to place our discoveries into the public domain, for the benefit of all.

One of the primary reasons this book is being written now is to provide this information as quickly as possible to as many people as possible who wouldn't have access to it otherwise. If the climate crisis predictions are true, and I have no reason to doubt they are, we need all hands on deck, all the tools we can muster, and all the possibilities for transformation explored.

I'm inspired by and consider myself part of the unofficial lineage of

Terence and Dennis McKenna and their good friend Dr. Rick Strassman, who is credited with reinitiating the Psychedelic Renaissance. In 1976, Terence and Dennis published a book under pseudonyms on how to grow psychedelic mushrooms, called *Psilocybin: Magic Mushroom Grower's Guide*. The *Ace of Buds* image on page xvii is a tribute to this lineage and was inspired by the McKenna brothers' *Ace of Shrooms* image featured at the beginning of their book. Growing your own psychedelic mushrooms is now a common psychedelic community experience. I wish for that openness, sharing, and empowerment with cannabis as a psychedelic and to do my part in breaking down the barricades to legal psychedelic healing.

Although this work isn't yet in the realm of research, it can definitely be considered a summary of practices I've found effective for healing. In a sense, these are notes from a scientific research expedition, not a research experiment. Is this the final word or expression? No. This book is closer to a first step. Is it going to be improved by others? I believe so. For the scientists and skeptics, I invite you to test the conclusions explored here.

Statement on Open Science and Open Praxis with Psilocybin, MDMA, and Similar Substances

Preamble: The undersigned individuals and organizations work to advance the understanding and beneficial uses of substances called (among many names) psychedelics, hallucinogens, or entheogens. Our fields include medicine and traditional healing, medicinal chemistry and ethnopharmacology, psychopharmacology, neuroscience, psychology, counseling, religion, public health, and public policy.

From generations of practitioners and researchers before us, we have received knowledge about these substances, their risks, and ways to use them constructively. In turn, we accept the call to use that knowledge for the common good and to share freely whatever related knowledge we may discover or develop.

Therefore, in this work, we commit to the following principles.

If we engage with consultants, contractors, or suppliers, we will do so in ways that uphold these principles.

1. **Intellectual and scientific integrity**—We affirm that we report the truth as we find it, not as we or others might prefer it to be found. We will present disappointing or adverse results as well as affirming or encouraging ones. We will properly attribute the contributions of others.

2. **In service**—While we may need to be paid for our labor, we are called to this work in the spirit of service. We will place the common good above private gain, and we will work for the welfare of the individuals and communities served. We will strive to make our expertise and services available to all who may benefit from them, even those whose means are limited.

3. **Open science and open praxis**—We will not withhold, nor will we require others to withhold, materials or knowledge (experiences, observations, discoveries, methods, best practices, or the like) for commercial advantage. This does not preclude the appropriate management of raw data or the exercise of data exclusivity rights, but we will make those decisions for the common good rather than for private gain. Nor does this preclude reasonable and ordinary charges for our books, other media, software, materials, or professional services.

4. **Non-interference**—We will strive to place our discoveries into the public domain, for the benefit of all. If we have patents or patents pending, we will license that intellectual property, for no more than reasonable and ordinary administrative costs, to anyone who will use it for the common good and in alignment with these principles.

Read the entire document on the Council on Spiritual Practices website.

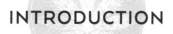

The Healing Gift
of Cannabis

I know it sounds impossible, but what if I were to tell you that there is a medicine—readily available and one that can be grown all around you—that can heal your trauma and wake you up to your true potential? What if I were to say that you didn't have to suffer as much anymore?

I have two daughters, and I find it hard to believe that this world we live in now is the best it will ever be. Will the wilderness of my youth be something beyond the imagination of my children? I believe it is a real tragedy that our children, through no fault of their own, are growing up in a world that, if left unaided, is going to be far worse in the future than it is today. The warning signs are all around us, and we're running out of time to change things for the better. I sincerely hope our goal is set a little higher than mere survival, but I'm not that confident. According to many reports on the climate crisis, we have about a decade to implement drastic change to advert global disaster.

But it's not just climate change we need to tackle. We need accessible and effective healing practices now, on the largest scale possible, so we can successfully respond to the daily struggles of a world in constant and ever-accelerating global paradigm shifts. In an age where collective trauma is rampant (and seems to only be getting worse), we need to reevaluate and assess all of the options available to us. *Cannabis sativa,* although previously overlooked, might be one of our best tools to implement psychedelic therapy on a large scale.

I used to think the large-scale version of this would be to train a corps of healers to go out and start facilitating groups with the medicine. And that is what we're doing. But what if we don't have time for even that? What if we need to take our healing into our own hands now? Not just for us now but to make it through the wild times ahead. This is the purpose of this book.

We desperately need to acknowledge we're living through a global pandemic of trauma during a period of extreme global transformation, and we need to actually do something significant and far outside the norm to address it. Here are just a few examples of the radical global transformation we're living through at the moment:

- Climate change and large-scale climate disasters
- Income and racial inequality
- 3D printing and decentralized manufacturing
- DNA recoding, designer babies, and immortality
- Organic agriculture and factory farming
- Nanotechnology
- The internet and virtual reality
- The corporate takeover of the psychedelic revolution
- Artificial intelligence, the singularity, and the post-job economy
- Energy revolution
- Corporate vs. nation-state conflicts
- Higher dimensionality and quantum computing
- Large hadron collider
- War, war, war, and more war
- Stolen elections and post-democracy America or peaceful progressive transformation
- Space travel and the possibility of extraterrestrial life
- Decline of religion and rise in spirituality
- Fukushima and other human-caused disasters

- Border security and climate crisis migration
- The rise of delusional conspiracy and "alternative facts"
- Global pandemics

In addition to the need for healing because of all these crazy happenings, we also need accessible psychedelic tools to support the development of increased resilience for the activists, veterans, first responders, mental health specialists, and other professionals on the front lines of our unhealthy collective choices. We need accessible psychedelic tools for the innovators and visionaries who help move our society toward greater health and vibrancy and away from unhealthy, unsustainable, and dangerous paths like militarism, nationalism, and the tragic destruction of our environment.

While the recognized psychedelics like psilocybin and LSD clearly possess this potential, our desperate societal needs are proving difficult for the psychedelic community to meet on the scale required, not only due to the trauma caused by fifty years of significant and continued prohibition (not to mention the slow and tedious process of legalization through clinical research and medical application) but also our collective ignorance of one of the most important tools that has been growing right in front of us. Most psychedelic medicines aren't yet legal. Cannabis is legal in a lot of places *right now*.

Yes, contrary to popular belief, *Cannabis sativa* is a classic psychedelic, and it can be used just as other psychedelics can be used. I know this because I facilitate psychedelic cannabis sessions all the time with people, and I have experienced the results firsthand.

The collective psychedelic community has minimized this sacred plant and relegated it to a position as either solely recreational or used as an adjunct to other medicines. Cannabis isn't considered a "real" psychedelic, and some in our medicine communities shame others for using it. Most of our eyes are fixated on the shinier, sexier psychedelics as the "right" ones to use, and somehow cannabis is the "wrong" one.

Many of us have a complex history with the medicine, as well—

getting caught smoking pot or being shamed for our curiosity about it is often one of the first traumatic psychedelic experiences many of us have as teens and younger adults. While our first experiences using cannabis are often the most magical, they're disregarded as dangerous and delusional, and the magic is shut down by others who don't understand. It's no wonder we have such a complex relationship with this plant medicine.

I've smoked cannabis for a long time, but my first real memory of recognizing the true psychedelic potential was about ten years ago in graduate school. I was attending Naropa University to receive my master's degree in transpersonal counseling psychology. I had every intention of becoming what's called an underground therapist, someone who used psychedelic medicines for therapeutic healing purposes. I had talked my program into letting me complete a body-centered mindfulness practice to fulfill a course requirement. As part of the practice, I was stretching in the spare bedroom of my apartment we used as a meditation studio. I'd smoked a copious amount of some really wonderful flower and was in a very deep, meditative state. I was gently stretching my neck when something released with a pop. I had my eyes closed, and I didn't just feel, but saw a yellow bolt of lightning quickly shoot up my spine to the top of my head. I thought, "Hmm . . . That was really interesting," and didn't think much of it after that. But looking back, I think that was the moment I first noticed the psychedelic potential of this medicine.

My buddy Jon knew of my interest in psychedelic therapy, as I'd sat in sacred spaces with him a number of times. I was trying to figure out how to make a living doing something I cared about deeply but was illegal to do, and by that, I mean being a healer and guide who uses psychedelics, without actually breaking the law. (I was married to my wife, Alison, by then, and we were thinking of having our first child.)

He said, "Hey, Daniel, have you ever considered using pot as a psychedelic? Like using it with the other practices you do?"

And I thought for a second and said, "No, I actually haven't."

And he replied, "You do know cannabis is a psychedelic, right?"

I said I did, but I had never really considered it.

Why was that? Something about not recognizing cannabis for what it was piqued my curiosity.

Jon said, "Hey, I want to help you try it out. Let's do it. I'll pay for the space, and let's see what happens."

I said okay, and that was the genesis of our Conscious Cannabis Circles.

The power of the medicine quickly became apparent to everyone who participated in the practice. I was quite skeptical about it, and if I'm being honest with myself, I still am sometimes. After more than seven years, though, I have yet to find the limits of the potential of this sacred plant.

It is really hard to describe what was happening to me through that time. I was being introduced to the psychedelic potential of a medicine completely overlooked by society and the psychedelic community. When Jon and I started this work, cannabis had been so degraded by the War on Drugs, and prohibition, and fear, and shame, and prisons, and its association with addictive drugs and the gateways to them that we just couldn't see it for what it was anymore. It was becoming more and more obvious that we had been lied to not only about how bad it was but also about how amazing this plant really could be as a tool for psychedelic therapy.

We had been taught to believe from an early age that pot is bad. People who use pot are unhealthy. Drug users. Immoral. So we lived in this numb life, with numbed pains, and the antidote to this pain was literally growing out of the earth all around us. We were so blind; we couldn't see the obvious. We even demeaned it. We called it a weed. I used it, even with respect, but I still didn't really see it.

But there was something about the process of exploring cannabis intentionally that continually inspired me to go deeper into the exploration of it. It felt like an *invitation* into a mystery and a puzzle to be solved and shared. So, I got to work experimenting with the potential of the medicine. I was intuitively drawn to blend strains and over a series of trials and errors and beginner's luck maybe—and could I have even been guided?—I found that I could mimic other psychedelic experiences with just plain ol' pot. And I don't mean sort of mimic. I mean truly mimic the potency and transformational power of other psychedelic medicines.

I was confused. Everything I knew about this plant was wrong. All the things I had minimized were its greatest gifts. How in the world was this happening? In the beginning, I was too inspired to really care about the *how*. I just wanted to see how far we could take it.

So we did. I experimented and experimented and experimented. I worked with my friends and anyone else who would let me, and something very special and very promising started to happen. Again and again, it happened. People around me started to heal deep trauma and wake up. I started to heal, too. I started to wake up.

Imagine a space of pure self-acceptance and full, deep awareness where you can see through your life, all the way back, at the things that happened, and realize that yes, they happened, but the meaning of them had changed into empowerment and understanding. A common experience after someone has healed deeply held trauma is for them to recognize and say: "I had to go through that struggle. I understand that now. I see the gifts that it gave me and I accept who I am because of it."

What does it really look like to help each other heal? And how might cannabis play an integral role in that healing process? This book sets out to explore the answers to those questions.

The purpose of this book is pretty simple. I would like to teach you exactly how to turn cannabis into a real psychedelic medicine and how to safely and effectively use it for healing and transformation. Within that simple intention are some major implications. In a very real sense, this is my attempt to help break through the barriers to using psychedelic medicines not only for healing but for all the other reasons we use psychedelics: to help solve problems and explore possibilities.

Part 1 provides an overview of our current state of affairs with cannabis, its legality, and its characteristics as a psychedelic medicine. I discuss the Medicinal Mindfulness orientation and how we use cannabis as a tool for psychedelic therapy. As a transpersonal psychedelic therapist, I also speak to its nature as a plant ally because I think this nomenclature and identity captures the mystery of psychedelic cannabis experiences, one far deeper than statistics and solely scientific discussions can probe.

In part 2, I share exactly how to make a psychedelic cannabis blend. I've discovered a few secrets, and I'm not keeping these secrets to myself. I'm finding that it is hard to be a part of a professional field no one else works in, and I'm starting to get lonely out here on the psychedelic cannabis frontier.

Part 3 provides the meditative tools and knowledge to prepare for the psychedelic cannabis experience. Cannabis is the safest psychedelic but using it doesn't come without risks. While I do recommend working with a therapist or a guide, for the vast majority of us, this just isn't possible. It's time to take the responsibility for healing into our own hands, not to wait for other psychedelic medicines and MDMA to become legal. Yes, these will definitely be beyond useful when they enter the mainstream, but we don't have a moment to lose.

In part 4, I speak about Cannabis-Assisted Psychedelic Therapy, methods for engaging the use of psychedelic cannabis for healing and creative problem-solving, as well as psychedelic exploration. These practices were developed over the past five years to amplify the psychedelic nature of cannabis. We begin from the perspective of the new user, then move into safely working with cannabis for the very first time, and finally discuss advanced journeywork practices for trauma resolution and advanced psychedelic journeywork techniques. These practices will help anyone translate greater skill and agency from psychedelic cannabis experiences to any psychedelic medicine experience.

Lastly, in part 5, I discuss the greater societal-level implications of these practices, how to implement these experiences into a safe, ongoing protocol for lasting change, and what tools you need to keep the process going in solo practices as well as in community groups.

Healing can happen now. We don't have to wait. We just have to look outside the box of what we were told is possible. The good news is you don't have to take my word for it. All of the practices discussed here can be tested and verified through personal experience.

PART ONE

Path of Gentle Power

❖ ❖ ❖

Contrary to popular belief, *Cannabis sativa* is a classic psychedelic, equal to psilocybin, LSD, ayahuasca, and DMT and even able to mimic the healing capacities of the empathogen MDMA. Not only that, but it might just be the most accessible and effective psychedelic medicine we have available for healing and transformational practices. It is certainly the most legal.

Psychedelics are amazing substances that elicit awe-inspiring and soul-transforming experiences. They simultaneously heal trauma and awaken human potential. Psychedelics are embedded within our culture on a nearly cellular level. Even if you have never taken psychedelics, your life has been greatly influenced by them (look no further than your smartphone), and as the resurgence in psychedelic interest continues to unfold, many people are looking for a safe introduction to the medicine. And for this we have to look no further than cannabis, the one psychedelic that is now legal for most Americans to consume.

Most of us associate cannabis experiences that are psychedelic in nature with eating too many edibles and getting sick, having panic attacks, and tripping really hard and very badly. Afterward, we rightly think, "Why in the world would I do that again?" But this common experience proves that even if it was a bad trip, it was a trip nonetheless.

What if we could skillfully use cannabis in a specialized form to minimize the undesirable effects of a psychedelic cannabis experience, such as anxiety and paranoia, and increase the positive effects, such as deep physical relaxation and an elevated healing state? What would the true potential of cannabis be in an intentional and healing context?

What if we have just collectively forgotten how to use cannabis for healing? What would happen if we integrated what we now know about psychedelic medicine therapies into a cannabis-specific practice? Would it be as effective as other psychedelic medicines in healing trauma? If so, what if we could teach people how to heal on their own?

In my practice, I use cannabis to elicit therapeutic psychedelic experiences in groups and individual settings, and it works consistently to evoke real psychedelic states. Most skeptics come out of a psychedelic cannabis experience with me completely surprised by the intensity of their trip, and it's not uncommon for even veteran psychonauts to report having the most intense psychedelic experiences they've ever had using any medicine, let alone just smoking pot.

Ayahuasca and DMT practitioners regularly say the cannabis experience is equivalent to these medicines. This can be summed up in the words of one of my participants, which express a common theme we encounter in the work: "The Conscious Cannabis Circle rivaled experiences I've had with the most potent psychedelics. I wouldn't have thought it possible had I not experienced it firsthand." Here's another one I received recently: "Having been a faithful cannabis user for most of my life, I approached my experience with Daniel with a good dose of skepticism. Turns out this was one of the most powerful experiences of my life. I found the cannabis medicine to be an extraordinarily versatile, intelligent, and kind ally."

We will further explore the characteristics and effects of this kind ally here in part 1.

Characteristics of
Psychedelic Cannabis

This book isn't a primer on cannabis. Those have been written. You don't need to know the details of the plant to use it as a psychedelic medicine. But I do want to share some context for those who might not have used it in a while as well as for those who have never used cannabis. If you're doubting whether it's possible for cannabis to create a psychedelic experience, consider when you last smoked it—a year, a decade, or a generation ago?

Simply stated, according to recent studies, the tetrahydrocannabinol (THC) in cannabis is three times stronger than it was twenty years ago. In addition, the percentage of the cannabinoid cannabidiol (CBD), also found in the plant as a natural antidote to THC, is decreasing in most strains through selective breeding. This means the subjective effects of the THC are felt even more strongly. We are literally witnessing firsthand the evolution of an entire species by human engineering and genetic manipulation.

The new scientific exploration of the relationship between cannabinoids (the active compounds of cannabis) and terpenes (its aromatic compounds) is called the *entourage effect,* and it has amplified the diverse qualities of cannabis through breeding subtle changes in chemical composition. Because of this new understanding, it's very safe to say cannabis today is nothing like it was two decades ago, let alone during the psychedelic '60s. I am sure there were some incredible exceptions to this trend, as there have always been wonderful growers of this amazing plant, but on average, exceptional cannabis wasn't the experience of the vast majority of users. Maybe it's time to reconsider this humble flower and its unusual smelling terpenes, which are like little engines of transformation.

Despite the strength of modern strains, cannabis is still honored in the healing community for its therapeutic nature. Because psychedelic cannabis sessions are shorter and recovery time is minimal, integration is easier than it is for other psychedelic medicines, which makes it ideal for those who have busy careers and family responsibilities. Psychedelic cannabis is also much safer for older people to use because it not only causes less stress on the body but is actually neuroregenerative in nature. Imbibing cannabis with intention is a natural harm-reduction tool as well, with regular users reporting that when they transitioned to intentional use and actually began to turn toward what needed healing, their overall cannabis consumption and other drug use decreased significantly and without much effort or clinical intervention. As an addiction treatment, cannabis is a much safer alternative to addictive drugs in the initial stages of treatment, and cannabis protocols and breathwork techniques can be used as tools to heal the underlying causes of addictive behavior. Except for a few easy-to-assess contraindications, there are few reasons not to promote this medicine for personal healing.

Cannabis is also much safer, psychologically and physically speaking, than any other psychedelic medicine, and it has a shorter duration than most psychedelics, making it easier to integrate and recover from the experience. It can be used effectively in smaller doses or as a way to step into working with other psychedelics. This is something we call "testing the waters." If you have never tried a psychedelic, there may be a few steps to take before going to Peru for a legal ayahuasca experience.

Unlike other psychedelics and MDMA, which require significant time between sessions for integration and physical well-being, cannabis can be used safely and on an ongoing basis for healing purposes, even weekly within the appropriate context. This book describes what that container could look like for a solo practitioner. In addition to safe ongoing use, as people become more skillful, they can gather together for community events. We regularly host more than twenty-five people in our circles. I'm not saying start with that, but community really is part of the medicine.

Subjectively, when used skillfully, psychedelic cannabis experiences are not that different from MDMA-assisted psychotherapy. The healing effects, including the intensity level of emotions, somatic release, and physical shaking as well as traumatic memory recall in a safe and accepting state of being, are sometimes indistinguishable from that of MDMA and other psychedelics. From my experience, psychedelic cannabis experiences often begin like MDMA sessions, then morph into something akin to a psilocybin mushroom experience with significant body sensations and vivid inner visuals. A very significant number of clients also state they experience ayahuasca- and DMT-level trips, especially if we add certain simple breathwork practices to the experiences.

Cannabis sativa is a safe and sacred medicinal tool that supports us in turning inward, resolving tensions stored deep within the body, tracking inner sensations, and releasing traumas from the nervous system. Using cannabis intentionally is completely different than getting high and escaping your problems.

THE PSYCHEDELIC CANNABIS EXPERIENCE

The psychedelic cannabis experience is a synergistic fusion of a full-spectrum *Cannabis sativa* blend with set, setting, and skill (primarily music, somatic awareness, and breath), within a multiparadigm, facilitated process that mimics a fusion of MDMA and psilocybin and often reaches ayahuasca- and DMT-level states, particularly when combined with gentle breathwork practices.

The psychedelic cannabis experience does not require extremely high doses but is exponentially stronger than an experience typically associated with cannabis alone. Experiences with psychedelic cannabis, however, generally exhibit far more personal agency than other strong psychedelic medicines. The peak of the experience can be modified to reach different intensities based on dosage and to last about one to three or more hours.

Cannabis is legal in most of the United States, can be safely used frequently for ongoing psychedelic therapy and psychedelic exploration purposes, and may be as effective as other psychedelic medicines for treating significant clinical disorders if placed in an appropriate protocol.

The following list provides some of the general psychedelic cannabis effects.

- Increased awareness of the physical body, often creating a form of synesthesia that combines our visual perception with proprioception, which is called *visual proprioception* in the Medicinal Mindfulness model
- Deep muscle relaxation leading to energetic discharges and trauma resolution, including the activation and clearing of the meridian and chakra channels, facilitating energy movement throughout the body and profound new levels of nervous-system regulation
- Capacity to travel through memory; increased awareness of mental habits, judgments, and anxieties leading to resolutions of unhealthy processes
- Deeper awareness of emotional processes and activation of emotional discharges, leading to release and healing
- Active, dreamlike, inner visual experiences and a clear capacity to imagine in a hypervivid inner reality
- Extreme creative problem-solving activation and increased connection to intuition
- Transpersonal phenomena such as visitations from entities or

aspects of self that feel apart from the self (ancestors, guides, angels, totems, etc.) and deep spiritual states of being and nonbeing that more closely resemble unity consciousness and profound connections with the Divine

- Activation of synchronistic transformational growth experiences in the external (real world) field that must be engaged by the journeyer
- A deep sense of presence and body awareness as opposed to being dissociative or "out there" or "somewhere else"
- Development of a sense of agency in life, feeling more in control of life situations and having more choice and feeling a deeper connection with the world and a greater sense of purpose

While we're on the topic of understanding what psychedelic cannabis is, I'd like to discuss why I've chosen to call it such. After exploring terms like *transcannabis,* denoting something that "transcends but includes cannabis," and *conscious cannabis,* which primarily denotes intentional use of cannabis as a mindfulness tool, I've currently landed on the simple and direct *psychedelic cannabis* to describe the medicine and the experience as something different from recreational consumption, otherwise known as "smoking pot."

Given the current dialogue on cultural and spiritual appropriation, I'd like to request that we be mindful of the words we use to describe this medicine as well—words like *ganja* from Hindu traditions, and as I've heard it referred to more recently, *Santa Maria,* a name associated with religious use of the medicine in Central and South America. Personally speaking, I don't believe these are my words to use. I most often describe it as simply "cannabis" or call it by its scientific name, *Cannabis sativa.* Because psychedelic cannabis is so new, we have an opportunity here to redefine our relationship with this medicine in terms appropriate for today's multicultural society.

PSYCHEDELIC CANNABIS
SCIENTIFIC CASE STUDIES

While cannabis research in clinical settings is limited by the quality of government cannabis and artificial prohibitions set up by the DEA, we've been able to conduct some experiments to explore the potency of psychedelic cannabis and see how it compares to other psychedelic medicines. We've conducted a few psychedelic cannabis sessions with participants hooked up to an EEG machine, and we've conducted an altered states questionnaire, also known as the Altered States of Consciousness Rating Scale (OAV), in a large group setting. While both experiments were very preliminary, the results were surprising and inspiring.

At a recent Psychedelic Sitters School training, the brainwave activity of two students was measured with an EEG machine before and after a Conscious Cannabis Circle. The two subjects tested both showed significant decreases in activity in the default mode network (DMN). The DMN is important because it is related to the mind's tendency to think about itself and is considered by many to be the seat of the ego or identity.

Psychedelic medicine literature has consistently demonstrated that subjects in a psychedelic state show decreased EEG activity across all bands, except gamma, in the default mode network. This suggests that the patterns observed in the Conscious Cannabis Circle case studies are similar to the EEG changes observed in research done with other psychedelic medicines, including LSD, psilocybin, and ayahuasca.

According to the literature, typical cannabis consumption that is more akin to recreational use consistently results in increased alpha activity, yet alpha activity decreased in both case-study subjects. A decrease in alpha wave activity is also consistent with research of other psychedelic medicines. Both subjects in this study demonstrated an EEG pattern that is contrary to typical responses to cannabis consumption.

Future research should explore EEG changes in a variety of cannabis-related experiences as well as the use of these experiences for therapeutic gains.

A second experiment is even more striking. I recently facilitated two Conscious Cannabis Circles in San Francisco, with twenty-six participants in each. Of these fifty-two participants, thirty-two filled out the OAV. Thirty-three percent of the participants were nonwhite, the average age was thirty-six, and the gender makeup was about evenly split, with fifteen females, fifteen males, one transgender participant, and one gender nonconforming participant. There was no control group.

While there is some debate about how accurate the OAV scale is in measuring psychedelic experiences, this is what we had to work with. The forty-two-question survey places the answers in the following categories: experience of unity, spiritual experience, bliss, insight, disembodied, impaired cognition, anxiety, complex imagery, elementary imagery, synesthesia, and changed meaning.

We then compared the results to the same survey conducted during a collection of MDMA, psilocybin, and ketamine research studies as outlined in a paper published in 2010 called "Psychometric Evaluation of the Altered States of Consciousness Rating Scale (OAV)" written by Eric Studerus, Alex Gamma, and Franz Vollenweider. (Refer to the graph on the next page.) While our results are by no means a peer-reviewed study, the survey measurements are significant. The measurements of the psychedelic cannabis survey were on average *twice* as high as the MDMA, psilocybin, and ketamine results, except in the categories of impaired cognition and anxiety, both of which were about the same as these other medicines. I've attempted to find the same information for ayahuasca and DMT to compare psychedelic cannabis to but have so far been unsuccessful.

What does this outcome mean exactly? I've checked the actual data more than once, and these are the results of our survey as compared to the results of the others. Our data set is significantly smaller and without a control group. Is psychedelic cannabis really twice as powerful as these other medicines in unity, bliss, insight, spiritual, and disembodied experiences, complex and elementary imagery, synesthesia, and changed meaning? I don't honestly know, but these results are consistent with many of the experiences that I have had on psychedelic cannabis and are consistent with many of the experiences my clients have reported. My psychedelic cannabis experiences may not have been twice as strong as the strongest psychedelic trip, but they have easily been as potent. More research is clearly needed to explore the real potential of psychedelic cannabis compared to other psychedelic medicines.

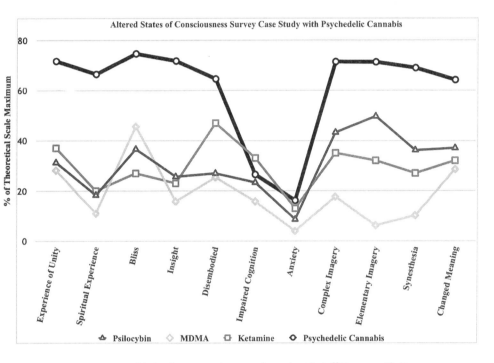

Source: Unpublished case studies conducted with Jeff Tarrant, Ph.D., NeuroMeditation Institute.

2

The Primary Differences between Cannabis and Other Psychedelics

If cannabis is used skillfully and within the right setting, there are several important and unique characteristics that make a psychedelic cannabis experience different from other psychedelics. Again, I am not discussing lower-dose, or psycholytic, experiences but full psychedelic experiences using cannabis. Even when extremely intense, the psychedelic cannabis experience appears to be more accessible and less overwhelming for our ego. We are better able to engage with and navigate through the experience with psychedelic cannabis than with other intense psychedelics, and this increases the potential for post-session integration. The primary difference between psychedelic cannabis experiences and other psychedelic experiences is one of agency and continual consent. Though we regularly report a greater feeling of control, it doesn't mean we're making the experience up but rather that we have a much greater capacity to engage our experiences with skill and intention than we typically would with other psychedelics.

Contrary to most psychedelic experiences where one feels a loss of control, cannabis allows us to regain and explore a new sense of agency. The development of personal agency has often been described as a key factor in trauma resolution and significant healing for my clients. Trauma, remember, is so often associated with a loss of control; thus, part of the resolution of trauma involves regaining control/agency. Unlike other psychedelics, cannabis gently invites us into deeper and deeper spaces and permits us to go at a chosen pace and in a chosen direction. At any time, we can even *pause* the experience by shifting our physical position or removing the eye covering to go to the bathroom, for example, or if it becomes overwhelming. This can't be said for any other psychedelic. If someone sat up from a DMT experience, they would clearly still be in it. With cannabis, that same person could sit up and would simply feel a shift to the sensation of being really, really high. Paradoxically, however, psychedelic cannabis journeyers generally choose not to pause the experience because it feels so safe and within their capacity to navigate. Thus, they continue to sink deeper and deeper into extremely evocative and peak psychedelic states but in a way they have chosen. No other psychedelic allows for this sort of pausing and titration.

I'm currently speaking of vaped or smoked cannabis when I speak of psychedelic cannabis experiences and this sense of agency. It's important to acknowledge the potency of edible cannabis and the higher likelihood of taking a dose that causes one to lose agency. This could manifest as a full range of experiences from a positive ego dissolution to a negative overdose-type experience including panic, paranoia, and vomiting. While it's possible to explore edibles that elicit agency, additional research on edible products seems required at this time, so it's not something we're going to discuss here. There are alternative edible options, though, if smoking or vaping isn't right for you.

I question the idea that the typical loss of control associated with psychedelics is part of the healing process or inner hero's journey. For someone seeking help healing their trauma, loss of control can be detrimental to the process because losing our sense of agency is often a primary cause of trauma to begin with. Having a choice on how the healing unfolds appears to be another important path to healing for us to consider as psychedelic therapists. This agency may be intimately connected with the healing itself as a corrective experience to a traumatic event.

Interestingly, cannabis can be used as a tool to develop and practice agency within other psychedelic states. Once developed within the context of psychedelic cannabis sessions, the skill of agency translates to other psychedelic medicines (not to mention day-to-day living), giving us more capacity to skillfully respond to deeply significant psychic material, somatic experiences, and opportunities in our lives.

Body awareness, along with a specific form of somatic healing, seems to be uniquely amplified with cannabis. Cannabis seems to address deeply held traumas in the fascia, tendons, muscles, and bones, as well as in our nervous systems, brains, memories, and emotional structures. This trauma is often discharged through trembling and shaking. In my experience, the body often needs time in between sessions to fully integrate the shifts brought about by these somatic releases, so I'd like to encourage you to relax into them, let them happen spontaneously and don't physically move to adjust out of the discomfort.

I often ask my clients probing questions about the physical and energetic symptoms of the experience to help them remain curious about them, and I'm going to teach you about that as well. Usually, if an emotional release happens through memory recall or spontaneous crying, I simply encourage the client to gently stay with the experience until it passes. This is an easily developed skill set. After the difficult processes end, we then get to explore the underlying gifts of understanding or physical relief that often occur after a trauma is released. Clinically speaking, we're shifting out of post-traumatic stress into post-traumatic growth.

The body can store a significant amount of this psychic energy, and it can be physically and emotionally strenuous to go through strong energetic discharges. Therefore, having a healing session with a shorter duration appears to be a very effective healing tool for trauma. Duration is an interesting concept with cannabis, as the length of an experience can be programmed with much more flexibility than with other psychedelics and MDMA—especially when it is smoked or vaped—without losing effectiveness, whereas lower doses of MDMA or psilocybin will result in a shorter, lighter, less therapeutic experience. Cannabis sessions can be programmed to have a stable peak period from about one to three hours or more in length that can be as intense as full MDMA/psilocybin/DMT peaks (except with greater agency). These practices are easy to fit into any schedule.

Getting a full night's rest after a psychedelic cannabis session is quite common. Generally speaking, sleep isn't disturbed after these sessions like it can be with other psychedelics and MDMA, and most clients report being able to sleep much better than usual afterward.

In some ways, paradoxically, the orientation to successful healing in cannabis work quickly becomes more about the path itself rather than a final destination called "healed." Ongoing and greater relief is enough of a step for those who seek healing, and the goal of being healed no longer becomes the primary focus. In my healing practice, there doesn't seem to be a specific delineation between the healing process and waking up to our potential. From this perspective, the baseline psychological state of most humans, one of being just okay and productive, as a goal for healing post-traumatic stress disorder (PTSD) is quite a low standard—especially if we compare it to our potential for truly thriving, as revealed by these medicines. As mentioned, cannabis is unique among the psychedelics in that it can be used regularly and is therefore more easily and more safely incorporated into ongoing spiritual and self-development practices.

I'm becoming more and more convinced that cannabis, when used skillfully, may be as effective as MDMA in treating PTSD. This is an important area that requires further study, but frankly, we may not have the time to do the research first before the world needs it on a larger scale. I believe cannabis is the key to our personal and global healing.

3

Cannabis and the Law

Cannabis sativa, disguised as something other than a psychedelic, became the first psychedelic medicine to be fully legalized or made available for adult use by medical recommendation in most of the United States. Because the use of cannabis as a therapy is unrestricted by a medical protocol and doesn't require a therapist or guide or a religious context to be legal for most Americans, it may be a model for other psychedelic legalization movements. Recently, two ballot measures to decriminalize or legalize psilocybin were passed in Denver and Oregon, and the Decriminalize Nature movement is expanding across the country. As of today, fifteen states and Washington, D.C., have legalized recreational cannabis, and nearly half of all states have legalized medical cannabis. Even the deep-red state of Oklahoma legalized medical cannabis in the 2016 election.* We could be seeing the legalization of cannabis on the federal level in just a few years.

According to the Pew Research Center, 67 percent of Americans supported the legalization of cannabis in November 2019,† and since the wins of the November 2020 election to legalize cannabis, 72 percent of the U.S. population has access to, or are currently gaining access to some form of legal cannabis.‡ Of these 234 million people, over 97 million

---

*See "Map of Marijuana Legality by State," DISA Global Solutions website.
†Andrew Daniller, "Two-Thirds of Americans Support Marijuana Legalization," (November 14, 2019), Pew Research Center Fact Tank website.
‡This percentage was calculated by adding the populations of states with some form of legalization and comparing it to the total U.S. population.

have full access to recreational cannabis without medical restrictions. Canada, with a population of 36.7 million, has also fully legalized and regulated cannabis for adult consumption at the federal level. Forty-six countries have now fully or partially legalized cannabis use.

Cannabis is a gateway medicine but not at all in the way people perceive it to be. We are told it's a gateway to addictive drugs and a downward spiral into oblivion. This couldn't be further from the truth. Cannabis is a powerful medicine, yes, but it is actually a gateway to healing, ecology, and global transformation. It's just that there's this big, rusty, chained-up gate called "Prohibition and Ignorance" blocking us from this potential. The makers and guards of that gate are the same people leading us to our real oblivion: a global ecocide for nothing more than short-sighted profits. We do not need to seek permission from these people for our own healing. If you're a fighter, fight like hell to legalize this medicine. The world needs it. Don't back down. Help us break down the gate to healing and freedom.

This work builds on that of countless others who have labored to break down that gate, and while there is still a long way to go in fully dismantling prohibition, laws and social norms are changing. And it is because of these activists that I was able to freely explore the full potential of this medicine. This lineage, the community spirit of this plant, and the most recent and devastating predictions on climate change are why I chose to write this book, to share with you what I've learned so far. I doubt it's the final word by any means, but I hope it will at least be useful.

If cannabis is legal in your state, you're an adult, and you make it through the safety self-assessment in chapter 14, there is really no reason not to try these practices. No FDA approval processes are required, and where it's recreationally legal, neither are recommendations from medical professionals, just novel adaptations of existing medical or recreational cannabis laws. Simply put, cannabis makes psychedelic healing *legal and available right now*. It is very safe to step into a solo practice, and I'd like to show you exactly how to do it.

If you're living in a state where it's not yet legal to use cannabis, it's okay to move if you must. We have whole communities of families that have moved here to Colorado to help someone in their family—a sick child, for instance—to find relief. But others are moving, as well, because they are drawn to the mere possibility of a glimpse of something they seek.

4

The Perspective of Medicinal Mindfulness

Colorado, along with Washington, instituted legalized cannabis for adult use in 2014, and my organization, the Center for Medicinal Mindfulness, was the first to start facilitating legal psychedelic cannabis experiences in the United States. It quickly became obvious what we were getting into after one of our first experiential cannabis groups. One of my friends very seriously stated, "If I didn't know and trust you, Daniel, I would swear you put DMT in that!" We were all blown away and completely surprised by the intensity of the experience. I've since facilitated sessions for thousands of people in individual and group psychedelic therapy settings and journey experiences using special blends of the medicine. As I mentioned earlier, we call the groups Conscious Cannabis Circles and also offer a shorter version called the Cannabis Healing Meditation, specifically designed to help heal trauma and chronic pain. We also facilitate special breathwork experiences that are cannabis assisted.

These events gave me an opportunity to further develop the potential for cannabis to be used, like other psychedelics, in individual and small-group settings to treat trauma, post-traumatic stress disorder, and other common disorders such as depression, anxiety, grief, and feelings of meaninglessness. We've learned that by combining skillful cannabis consumption with the right therapeutic healing modalities and the right theory and experience, it's possible to reliably provide profound psychedelic experiences to clients while fully complying with the legal regulations of adult recreational and medical cannabis use.

The philosophy of Medicinal Mindfulness is unique in that we actively pull from safe-use strategies and journeywork techniques from all four primary contexts in which people use psychedelics: spiritual and religious contexts, psychological and therapeutic contexts, recreational and creative contexts, and contexts of intellectual curiosity and creative problem-solving. Working within this multiparadigm approach that incorporates the most important characteristics of each increases the intensity and effectiveness of the psychedelic cannabis experience and exponentially amplifies the psychedelic nature of the plant. Examples of these approaches include ritual; ceremony and prayer; somatically informed psychotherapies for trauma healing; breathing and mindfulness practices; knowledge of psychedelic theory and concepts developed through transpersonal psychology; playfulness; trust; curiosity; imagination; alchemy; depth psychology; the central importance of music; body posture; and many others. When these components are combined into a specific experience, the practice elicits its own entourage effect, not just from the chemical components of the plant but from the combination of the plant and the set and setting of the experience. These practices amplify the psychedelic effects of the medicine in rather profound ways, which in turn allow the medicine to be used for purposes common to other psychedelics, such as resolving trauma like MDMA can and eliciting mystical experiences like psilocybin can. It's a very *real* psychedelic experience.

This intentional use of the medicine explicitly adds a third dimension to the common psychedelic expression, "set and setting." In the Medicinal Mindfulness approach, we add the term *skill set* and have changed the saying to "set, setting, and skill." This explicit recognition of the skill sets we use allows us to develop them further. A psychedelic experience is no longer something that just happens to us; it's an experience to directly engage with. This simple shift in orientation leads to some pretty dramatic results and takes out the need for dogmatic belief systems. These practices can be tested and verified.

In the psychedelic cannabis experience itself, the Medicinal Mindfulness orientation subscribes to the commonly held principles of psychedelic therapy, most notably LSD researcher Stanislav Grof's concept of the *holotropic* nature of the human spirit—that given the right circumstances, we naturally move toward healing and empowerment. We also subscribe to Grof's idea that any difficult symptom in a psychedelic journey experience is something *halfway out* and that if we can accept it, relax around it, and allow it to move through us, then healing and understanding become natural byproducts of this process. A psychedelic therapist assisting a client with trauma, for example, simply encourages the client to stay in direct contact with the experience through acceptance and physical relaxation while urging them go deeper into their awareness of it. Generally, a client will report vibrations and/or tremors in their body, and we can visually observe their arms and legs trembling as the energetic, emotional releases are discharged.

Medicinal Mindfulness events became laboratories in which we combined cannabis with different therapeutic, mindfulness, and somatic modalities and noted the results. Through this process, we developed specific protocols to facilitate psychedelic therapy experiences for different purposes, such as healing trauma. The practices are informed by, but not limited to, clinical orientations, and this allows us to consider solutions outside the scope of clinical or medical modalities. What we've found is both simple and spectacular. Not only does psychedelic cannabis appear to be capable of effectively treating the same clinical concerns as other psychedelics, but as the program evolved, and I began to understand the process more completely, I started to wonder whether the therapist even needs to be there at all.

Current research studies on the efficacy of cannabis for the treatment of PTSD are severely limited by the quality of the medicine available through federally approved studies and only account for using the medicine itself as a form of symptom management through daily habitual use. There are no studies that combine cannabis and psychotherapy, and the term *cannabis-assisted* doesn't yet appear in psychedelic literature.

In the meantime, cannabis-assisted healing modalities like yoga, mindfulness, breathwork, massage, psychedelic therapy and psychotherapy, intentional community building, spiritual and religious use, and other novel applications aren't waiting for research scientists; they're actively being developed in thriving programs wherever cannabis cultivation, sale, and consumption is legal.

As much as we give thanks to this sacred medicine for providing immediate relief to severe suffering, the current research only scratches the surface of cannabis's potential to treat clinical disorders, physical injuries, and illness, especially when combined with somatic awareness, mindfulness practices, and trauma-informed psychotherapy interventions. The clinical approach to cannabis research also completely ignores the positive spectrum of psychedelic medicine use for the exploration of personal and collective potential and human development.

What if we could have it both ways? A practice that elicits trauma resolution while simultaneously waking us up to who we truly are and what we're called do in what the poet Mary Oliver calls our "one wild and precious life." What if it were a skill set teachable to others? And what if it could be implemented safely on a large scale, starting now?

The Emergence of Cannabis-Assisted Psychedelic Therapy

When I started working professionally with cannabis as a psychedelic in 2014, the term *cannabis-assisted psychotherapy* didn't exist as a defined healing modality. It was only recently, within the past few years, that cannabis has become more recognized as a potential tool for psychotherapy. That said, cannabis is still most commonly judged as a drug of abuse in the psychotherapist community. In fact, there are no references to the term in current cannabis-related publications and research papers. This doesn't mean people weren't benefiting from cannabis or having psychedelic experiences with it before, just that the term *cannabis-assisted* wasn't in the collective vocabulary.

According to recent research, about a third of medical cannabis patients use it to treat trauma, PTSD symptoms, and mood disorders like anxiety and depression, about a third use it to manage physical pain, and about another sixth use it to help with sleep.* Just using it like a daily medicine is enough to gain significant relief. But what if we could amplify the benefits of cannabis not only to provide relief but to elicit true and sustainable healing?

---

*Julie Weed, "New Study Shows Top Reasons That Patients Are Turning to Cannabis," (March 11, 2019), Forbes website.

I've developed a series of mindfulness practices and therapeutic techniques called Cannabis-Assisted Psychedelic Therapy; these techniques pertain to the use of cannabis as a psychedelic within the contexts of therapy, personal and spiritual exploration, and creative problem-solving. This method consists of a family of practices for personal empowerment, healing, and transformation, adapted in this book for solo use.

At the Center for Medicinal Mindfulness, Cannabis-Assisted Psychotherapy describes a subset of sessions that are generally shorter in duration (two to three hours) and have a specific clinical purpose. These types of sessions are more psycholytic in nature, meaning that they are like low-dose psychedelic sessions.

The purpose of this book is to share the knowledge base I've developed while exploring the healing potential of psychedelic cannabis. I've always considered it more of a guided mindfulness practice and a skill set that can be taught and further built upon rather than something simply *done* to a client by their therapist. While support is nice, it isn't always available. I'm living in one of the most privileged communities in the United States, particularly when it comes to access to effective healing modalities. Not everyone can find a psychedelic therapist or afford their services. I have a problem with that. I want to make this treatment accessible to those who have no accessibility. I want to share the medicine. This is the spirit of cannabis anyway—one of community, ecology, and sharing. How could I do otherwise?

One doesn't necessarily have to be a licensed, professional psychotherapist to skillfully self-heal using cannabis as a psychedelic. And frankly, so many of us have been struggling for so long, we'd be willing to take the chance . . . if only we knew how to do so.

6

Cannabis as a
Plant Spirit Ally

Without exception, we can trace every psychedelic medicine to a natural origin, a plant that can symbolize a sacred earthly spirit. Psilocybin is extracted from mushrooms, LSD from a mold, DMT from a root, ayahuasca from a vine and a leaf—the list goes on and on—but the psychoactive ingredient in cannabis is unique in that it originates in the nectar of a flower. For this reason alone, it would be an understatement to say we can associate cannabis with the sacred feminine. We call it a weed, but that just means it's so resilient, versatile, and abundant, it can grow anywhere. And just like the sacred bounty of the Great Goddess, its uses as a plant are too numerous to describe here. It heals the land just by growing there.

Cannabis has a plethora of spiritual imagery associated with it. In fact, many practitioners believe the medicine represents a *spirit ally,* and it's often experienced as such in a session. Even if this material is solely symbolic and not spiritual in nature, there are significant therapeutic reasons to engage this sort of psychic material in your sessions.

As a sacramental substance, cannabis is a symbol of the sacred feminine. To imbibe her is to worship and give praise to the Great Goddess, Mother of All Things. Historically speaking, cannabis is an ancient medicine. We, as a species, probably started smoking it as soon as we figured out how to smoke. Cannabis use is intertwined with multiple spiritual traditions and their development, and it's considered a sacred sacrament and healing herb. Some even associate the plant with the tree of life.

Cannabis's multitude of uses reflects its ability to mimic other medicines as a shapeshifter. It could therefore be represented as the many-faced Goddess: the maiden, the mother, and the wise grandmother. She is humble and down-to-earth, yet incredibly magical. She's a trickster, a contrarian, switching paths from one medicine experience to another, for example dancing between experiences akin to MDMA and psiloycybin, while gently testing our capacity to receive her healing. And humbly, she trusts us and our process and provides not just what we need, but exactly what we ask for. If you have a need, there's a cannabis strain to fulfill it; just ask any budtender in any Colorado dispensary.

Cannabis is a spell caster. She tricked the mainstream into thinking she was just another recreational drug. As part of her own heroine journey, she shape-shifted and degraded herself by pretending to be just like alcohol and opiates, all the while planting seeds of her master medicinal alchemy. This debasement was just a ruse and after medical cannabis became legal and then recreational, it became possible to once again explore her incredible potential without fear of persecution. This has led to a blossoming exploration of her true potential, not only as an allopathic medicine but also as a playful, creative, and rejuvenating intoxicant. This is evidenced by the green rush of entrepreneurial endeavors surrounding the cultivation and sale of cannabis, leading to new products for both pleasure and healing. This context has also led to the exploration of her potential as a psychological healing modality and a tool for spiritual exploration and development. She is her own path, but she loves working and playing with others, being a natural complement to yoga and meditation practices, the creative arts, and most notably, psychedelic exploration and psychotherapy.

Alchemically speaking, if LSD and MDMA, or ayahuasca and peyote, are the alchemical golds and silvers of the psychedelic family, then cannabis is the copper. If these same medicines are the brightest lights in the sky, the sun and the moon, then cannabis is the third-brightest light, the planet Venus, associated with the Goddess of Love and again symbolized by copper. If these medicines were the king and the queen, then cannabis would be the androgynous child, the fourth stage of alchemy, the sacred conjunction, fully realized and fully expressed and playful.

While it's true gold and silver are clearly more valuable than copper, ounce per ounce, are these metals really the most useful? How much copper runs through the walls of our homes? How much is in our computers? In a similarly humble service, cannabis may be the most useful and important psychedelic we have available. Like a good conductor, cannabis helps integrate, translate, and titrate the intensity of other psychedelic medicine experiences.

If ayahuasca is the archetypal Grandmother, then cannabis is the Mother, associated with infinite compassion, gentleness, nurturing, healing, and acceptance. Cannabis not only guides us with her wisdom like a mother, she also feeds us with her seeds and oil. We make both clothes and homes with her fibers. As a medicine, she brings comfort to children who can't stop shaking and to the parents who hold them during their epilepsy. This association with the Mother even exists at the molecular level with anandamide, an endogenous cannabinoid that is key to embryonic attachment to the uterus, as well as a natural cannabinoid in breast milk.

Cannabis is associated with awakening, symbolized by the destructive power of the Hindu Lord Shiva, helping us dispel illusion so we can become ourselves. Cannabis as the Lion is an ancient symbol passed down through Rastafarianism and ancient Hinduism representing power, courage, confidence, and pride.

Cannabis can be anything to anybody, and that's one of her greatest gifts to us. She helps both the young child with epilepsy and the elder with chronic pain and dementia. This is how we work with her as a psychedelic. We simply create the necessary preconditions, the right set and setting, and evoke the right mindfulness skills, then politely and graciously ask her to become psychedelic. She is gentle yet powerful in her desire to help us heal.

Things We Forgot to Dream About
In Gratitude

Hey, what if?

What if cannabis is a psychedelic?

If we can use it to heal trauma right now, before other psychedelics are legal?

What if we're just scratching the surface of the potential of cannabis?

What if it just gets better from here?

Would you do it?

Take the chance that your skepticism, although justified, is wrong?

What if we already have the technology to heal the world?

What if it's literally growing all around us?

We've just forgotten to dream about it.

What if?

What if we heal the trauma of the oppressors, so they no longer oppress?

Would we do it?

What if we could scoop up every broken heart and every broken soul and let them rest in the bosom of recovery and nurturing depth?

Would we do it?

All I can say is, thank you, Cannabis!

I've so enjoyed watching you grow and evolve these past seven years.

When prohibition is over, and we can spread you across the world,

it will clearly be a better place because of it.

PART TWO

Psychedelic
Cannabis Blends

Making Many Spirits One

◆◆◆

I am inspired by a future where all of humanity can effectively use psychedelic medicines, including cannabis, free from the fear of prosecution and the judgments of misunderstanding. I have seen too many beneficial results working with these treatments not to wish this for our world.

I sincerely believe if this were to happen, if these medicines were used on a large scale with intention, we would be able to heal the societal traumas that so deeply divide us. I sincerely believe we already have every solution for all of our problems and that the resolution of trauma is central to the possibility of not just surviving the next decades as a species but actually thriving during this transitional time instead.

One thing these medicines teach us is that these ideas, as idealistic as they sometimes sound, are not out of reach. How, then, do we live in a way to reach these potentials? If it were easy, wouldn't we have done it by now?

My answer to this dilemma is quite simple: we do all of the above. We absolutely need all the tools we can muster during this critical period for humanity. All hands on deck. No solution is too novel to explore. Yet, unfortunately, cannabis is one of the most unacknowledged vital resources of our community. It was instrumental in the founding of this country yet made completely illegal for the past fifty years. There has been incredible harm caused by prohibition. We can't really see this plant and its potential anymore. We've forgotten how to work with it.

This section explores a rediscovery of cannabis as a potent psychedelic. While many people acknowledge that cannabis can provide a meaningful psychedelic experience, there's very little discussion on the most skillful methods to utilize it as a psychedelic. There are still a number of professional identities that rely on a disingenuous misrepresentation of cannabis, either claiming it's a harmful drug or not a psychedelic at all. Both are wrong. Cannabis is a potent little flower.

In these next few chapters, I'll share with you central concepts on making psychedelic cannabis blends, how to prepare them, and everything I know so far about what constitutes the best blends for psychedelic journeywork, including my secret alchemical ingredient. After that, I'm going to teach you how to use cannabis to heal trauma and have really profound psychedelic experiences for personal healing and personal development practices.

One of my intentions in writing this book is to start a dialogue and receive feedback from readers to elicit valuable information that could more easily and more effectively explain these practices. I hope to plant some seeds here.

Cannabis Strains

I would like to invite you to put aside everything you think you know about this medicine, even if for just a moment. I am going to speak from my truth and share what I know. Everything I say here is verifiable through personal experience.

In practice, there is really no such thing as a singular *Cannabis sativa,* only cannabis *strains.* The effects of cannabis strains are so diverse that it's impossible to even begin to discuss them in this context. To oversimplify, if you have a need, there's a strain to address it. You need to sleep? Done. You need to stay awake and focus? Done. You need some pain relief? Done. You want to have fun? Done. Be creative? Done. The list goes on and on. The states of consciousness and physiological effects are extreme and very divergent. For that reason, there really is no such thing anymore as *just* pot. The equivalent would be like defining humanity through the filter of just one type of human, while ignoring the diversity of human cultures.

Each strain has a unique voice, a state of being that can resonate with each of us in the same way. These are the mind states they induce. Different strains, even different plants from the same strain, have vastly different voices. Where and how they are grown also greatly influences the voice of the plant; different light, different nutrients and soils, and different days of harvest all create the unique characteristics of the medicine. For these reasons, cannabis is a constantly evolving organism, and a strain grown in one area of the world will be vastly different from the same strain grown somewhere else or by someone else. Everything about it is in a constant state of change. As practitioners who choose to work with this medicine, we learn to adapt to this ever-evolving environment.

Though a lot of strains are described as psychedelic in their·effects, there really isn't a single psychedelic strain as defined here. It is actually far more complicated than that. The most advanced psychedelic states we can reach on this medicine are induced by blending multiple strains into a single cannabis experience.

THC, the active psychedelic molecule in cannabis, is only one factor in this plant's potential to affect us. We now know that the mind state induced by a particular strain is affected not only by other cannabinoids but also something called the *terpene profile,* the different chemicals in the medicine that make it smell and grow a certain way. THC is like the booster rocket, and the terpenes are like the navigation coordinates. The THC takes you there, but the terpenes determine where *there* really is. And by *there,* I simply mean a certain state of awareness.

Cannabis sativa strains are most commonly classified by the general states of awareness they induce, though there is a lot of variety within each category. The three main strain families include the *sativas,* which induce very altered, cerebral experiences but sometimes cause anxiety; the *indicas,* which increase body awareness and release body tensions but can also cause sedation; and the *hybrids,* which are often mischaracterized as a middle ground between sativas and indicas but could more accurately. be described as a third dimension of the plant and are heart opening or heart centered in their characteristic effects. Strains can also be characterized as having primary effects, such as increasing our ability to focus, explore creative states, enter deep relaxation, help us heal and recover in some way, or provide a boost of energy. From this perspective, even more subtle characteristics of strains can be discerned, including alterations to our perception of time and even the onset speed after inhalation.

Using the entourage effect of these families of chemical profiles, represented by the three primary strain types, it's possible to create what we call a full-spectrum psychedelic cannabis blend that elicits the best qualities of the different cannabis strains and reduces or eliminates their negative qualities. This integration of strains creates a unique *trans-cannabis,* or hypercannabis, mind state that incorporates all of the positive psychospiritual effects caused by the different terpene profiles in each of the unique strains used in the blend.

Again, when strains are combined, the positive qualities remain, while the negative qualities are balanced out and negated. For example, the anxiety-producing qualities of a sativa are balanced out and negated by the sedating qualities of the indica. At the same time, the sedating qualities of the indica are negated by the uplifting energy of the sativas. What remains is an uplifting, psychedelic experience with profound somatic awareness. The positive qualities of both strains—the creative introspection of the sativa and the greater body awareness of the indica—remain. The negative qualities of both strains—the anxiety of the sativa and the dull sleepiness of the indica—are significantly reduced. This somatic awareness and body relaxation in an elevated cannabis state are significant keys to trauma resolution. When we combine strains of the sativa and indica with a hybrid strain, a heart-opening, MDMA-like quality is allowed to emerge. Unlike the typical edible, higher doses of a blend are far safer because the negative qualities associated with the high, psychedelic-level THC dosing of edibles, such as panic and nausea, are negated by the blending of strains.

Currently, it's extremely important to work with the flower of the plant in its raw form, either smoked or vaped. Turning the flower into concentrates and oils often strips many of the terpenes out of the chemical makeup of the plant. While some terpenes remain, there are significant differences in the experience, and the absence of the full profile may be the primary factor in a blend being almost psychedelic but not quite. You can try increasing your dose, but that may lead to anxiety and even panic. The full-blown psychedelic states are easily reached with just the flower. In the end, you are going to use what you can find, and from experience, even nonpsychedelic cannabis strains combined with these practices are deeply healing. The primary determination of success is to keep engaging the process.

8

Going to the Dispensary

When it fits our schedules, I take my out-of-state clients to a Colorado dispensary, introduce them to the budtenders who work there, teach them about the different products, and have them smell all of the different jars of medicine. It is a really wonderful experience. Our Psychedelic Sitters School program includes a trip to the dispensaries specifically so people from other states can see how high quality cannabis can be. Don't settle for poor cannabis or bad business practices. As a consumer, you have a lot of power. Politely demand clean medicine. There's a general sense in Colorado that our methods to regulate and sell cannabis are working more often than not.

While there are more nuanced factors that affect the quality of a blend for psychedelic medicine purposes, it's important to consider the quality of the medicine. First and foremost, it's important to find and use organic sources, if at all possible. Too many growers use strong pesticides on their plants or don't know how to apply these chemicals properly and put them straight on the flowers people consume and smoke. Combining these chemicals with a flame is generally *not good*. Many of these chemicals have chronic negative effects. That said, these problems can mostly be avoided in a well-regulated market. Ask around and call dispensaries to learn more about their growing techniques. Learn to distinguish between good marketing and best practices. Become knowledgeable about the plants and the products used on them.

When you arrive at the dispensary, you'll be asked to show your ID and then brought into a back room with a selection of different edibles, concentrates, oils, hashes, candies, and jars upon jars of the raw flower. The first dispensary trips are like going into an adult candy store. It's easy to get lost in the selection. Have fun and experiment. Begin to incorporate cannabis into your life and get to know the medicine in its different capacities and forms. Follow the advice of the budtender you work with and start out very, very light. You're going to want to learn how the medicine affects you and at what dosages.

If high-quality cannabis is available, you're aiming for an average THC concentration above the range of 20 to 25 percent to make a great blend. CBD, even though a wonderful healing tool as a natural anti-psychotic and antidote to THC, should be avoided except with blends specifically used for cannabis-assisted massage therapy, yoga, and breath-work practices, which I'll discuss later. The budtender should know the percentages of THC and CBD in each strain, as they are required by law to be tested, but they may also have information regarding other cannabinoids and terpene profiles.

As much as I enjoy looking at the terpene lab results, I've found the best way to get the best medicines is to interview the budtenders and to trust my nose. I'm looking for certain qualities of awareness induced by the medicine, so I ask basic questions about the strain—whether it's an indica, sativa, or hybrid or where on that range it is and which ones they personally like the most and why. Often budtenders will know which one clients of the dispensary use for clinical issues such as pain, trauma, anxiety, depression, and poor sleep, all of which are common problems most of us have.

Take some time to smell the strains and get to know their terpene profiles. There are some incredible resources online that share informa-tion on terpenes and how they affect the body and mind. Or feel free to, like me, take a more intuitive approach and listen to your nose. It isn't always that the medicine you're looking for smells *good* but that it has a lot of complex fragrances within it. It's usually the case that something about the fragrance is *attractive* or *intriguing.* There's an invitation to get to know it more. When you make a purchase, it might be useful to buy small amounts of several strains so you can compare their effects. Once you find the strains you like, you can begin buying larger amounts to save some money and have a consistent strain to practice with. Take notes. Don't be surprised if the same strain at a later date, or from a different dispensary, has significantly different effects on your awareness.

Cannabis should always be stored in a dry, dark location. For the best care and results, remove all cannabis from plastic containers and place it in glass jars, if possible. Remember to label your jar so you don't lose track of the medicine. I like to keep notes about the medicine on the jar as well.

Before attempting to make a blend, get to know the medicine more by taking one or two small puffs and meditating with it. What do you notice about the changes in your body awareness? What do you notice about your attention? Your emotions? Does your heart rate increase? Do you feel sleepy? Does it do what the budtender said it would? Do you become anxious or paranoid? Sit with your eyes open, then closed. Do nothing or explore a task and see how the medicine affects the experience. I'll speak more about these practices in the next section of the book, but don't wait. Go have fun. Use a journal to keep track of your experience and what you notice.

While handling difficult experiences will be discussed later, I want you to know that this exploration is very safe. Start with small amounts of the medicine and work your way up to larger doses. Again, if you haven't smoked in a while, you might be surprised by the intensity of the medicine, even after just one puff. Take your time and wait at least ten minutes after the first inhalation before trying a second. The raw flower—vaped, not smoked—is the safest way to consume the medicine. Stay in a contained space and never drive after imbibing. Stay seated and be mindful when rising—sometimes standing up can make you lightheaded. Enjoy exploring the experience, and when you are ready to go deeper, you'll know. Listen to your favorite music. Write in your journal.

This practice alone can be very meaningful and deeply healing.

Making a Psychedelic Cannabis Blend

When I first started intentionally working with cannabis some years ago, I had no idea how special and unique its application as a psychedelic therapy really was. In some ways, the trajectory of my own life gave me all the pieces I needed to develop and amplify this medicine's potential far beyond anyone's expectations. I'll admit, in the beginning I was solely guided by my intuition. I don't even remember where the idea of blending the medicines came from. This is just something that made sense. It seemed obvious, and only later, after speaking to so many people, did I realize it wasn't.

I have been working professionally with this medicine full-time for more than five years. In this time, through experimentation and research, I've had the opportunity to really home in on a few important factors, and I've actually discovered an interesting secret about the blends I'll share with you in the next chapter. In a sense, I feel like a detective tracking a mystery, and I've been given clues along the way. But first, let's explore the medicines you'll immediately have available to you.

Making a cannabis blend is a very special experience. I fundamentally think of it as a sacred sacrament, and I put effort, care, and intention into making the blends. I sit in my meditation space, and I use a big mortar and pestle to mix the strains. Blending cannabis is a mindfulness practice in and of itself. I add the strains with prayer, smell each of them individually, and begin to grind up and mix the medicine. After a little while, I'll use a spoon to mix the medicine, chop up any clumps, and clean the mortar. I then go another round with the pestle. I repeat this process until the mix is pretty uniform, but not completely powdered. Powdered cannabis is harder to smoke because it blocks airflow. With simpler blends, a grinder and a spoon are enough, but if you're mixing a lot of medicine, the mortar and pestle is easier on the wrist and hands if the cannabis is dry enough.

I like to think this practice combines the many different personalities of each strain into one cohesive expression of the plant, which is transpersonal in nature in that these blends transcend individual strain experiences but rely on nothing more than the individual strains themselves. In Gestalt practices, this is often referred to the whole being greater than the sum of its parts. I call this practice "making many spirits one."

After I mix a new blend, I add the remainder of the older blend into the new one, then mix and grind them together just a little bit more. I personally believe that knowing the medicine from my very first journey, even in microscopic amounts, is still present in the blend I'm using adds meaning to the experience. I consider it a form of energetic lineage that adds significance to the work.

Making a full-blown psychedelic cannabis blend may not be immediately possible where you live, or it might take time to find the right allies and growers. Whatever the hurdle is, I encourage you to keep trying. Get to know local growers, activists, dispensaries, and other practitioners. Compare notes. Look for plants that are grown out of respect and love for the medicine. Though you might not get the results you're looking for right away, I've really learned to trust this medicine. Making a blend is like a hero's journey, an expedition of discovery. Sometimes it feels like these medicines find us as much as we find them. Work with what's available. Promote clean medicine practices. Educate your friends about what you're learning. Odds are, they're looking for it, too.

A good potential psychedelic medicine blend will include three basic strains of about equal weight—one-third sativa, one-third indica, one-third hybrid. You'll need a scale as some strains are denser than others, so although the amounts may look the same, their weights may be significantly different. If you can, develop your own relationship with different strains and experiment with different blends. Again, start with strains that smell right to you. It isn't uncommon to make a blend with six to nine strains, and I've even made blends with sixteen strains or more. Some blends are better than others, so it isn't about mixing just any strain. Each strain adds a certain quality that makes each blend unique. Different blends can be developed for different therapeutic purposes and in the future I expect that to be commonplace.

That said, you don't have to start with the most complex blends to get significant benefits from the medicine. And I know many people who have psychedelic experiences using a single strain when they combine it with the practices I describe in the next section. It's okay to feel frustrated if you hit some dead ends. Just don't stop trying.

The following descriptions offer different levels of psychedelic blends to get you started and include what I know about the most complex psychedelic blends I've made.

Level 1 blend—Start with a strain you already know you like to begin these practices. You really can't go wrong, and it's the safest way to get started for people new to cannabis or psychedelic healing practices. While community-created blends are available at our Conscious Cannabis Circles, we invite people to bring their own medicine, as well, should they choose to. It seems like everyone who brings their own medicine has deeply meaningful and healing experiences.

Level 2 blend—Make a two- or three-strain blend. Start with a strain you know you like, then look for its opposite. For example, if you enjoy a particular strong sativa, seek a strong indica to combine it with. There might be several options to choose from, so experiment. Make a blend with a single sativa and an indica in a 1:1 ratio. If you'd like to take the blend another step up, add a nice hybrid that you like the qualities of in a 1:1:1 ratio blend. This is the advice we give to participants of our circles who wish to bring their own blends. I can make recommendations for specific three-strain blends that I know work exceptionally well for these experiences. These blends have a good chance of being strongly psychedelic at higher doses but with a lower chance of difficult experiences.

Level 3 blend—Create more complex blends. Taking the general ratio of 1:1:1 for indicas, sativas, and hybrids, mix multiple strains together—two of each, or even three of each. Explore traits of certain strains you like and incorporate them into the blend. Look for extremely potent, anxiety-producing sativa strains and pair them with incredibly deep, relaxing, even sedating indica strains. Explore different combinations, different polarities of the medicine and how they affect your body. This can be a very intuitive, guided experience. Sometimes you may pick up different strains from different dispensaries or a particular strain from a friend's private garden. Get to know your community of cannabis consumers.

After you make a blend, keep good notes about it. If you like the blend you made, but it isn't quite right, what is it missing? Maybe you can adjust the ratio of the strains to refine the desired results. If you're too sleepy or drifty, add more sativa. If you're a little anxious, maybe add more indica. If you'd like to increase the emotional component of the experience, add more hybrid. With strains of nine or more, the ratios can eventually become quite complex.

Level 4—This is the Alchemy Blend, and it deserves its own chapter.

10

The Alchemy Blend

The Alchemy Blend is one of the more interesting stories of this expedition, and it is made from what I jokingly call my "secret ingredient." I jest about these blends being just pot, but in all honesty, even though there's something a little extra added to the Alchemy Blend, it's still made from only cannabis flower. While I like to play with paradox and polarities, it just so happens I discovered this one quite by accident.

One of the very first blends I made included some from a friend's private grow. It was a very high-quality indica with a strong THC content. It was a beautiful flower covered in crystals, so good that my buddy kept it tucked away for at least a year before I tried any of it. There was something very special about these initial blends I couldn't quite put my finger on.

Fast forward many months, and I'm visiting another friend who had gifted me a good amount of a particular sativa strain generally known as Blue Dream. It's a very popular strain, but I didn't know at the time Blue Dream was a sativa because the flower my friend gave me very much appeared to be an indica. Not only that, but I really felt the blends I made with it were just as good as those special ones in the beginning. They were very psychedelic and very rich in body experience. It seemed to add one more dimension to the experience, like going from 2D to at least 3D space. It was different.

I was sharing this phenomenon with a friend when we realized both strains from the different growers were quite old, aged at least six months to a year. The reason my second friend had given me so much of it was because it was from a previous harvest. We learned that through oxygenation and exposure to sunlight, over time, THC turns into another cannabinoid called cannabinol, or CBN. This was the secret ingredient I was looking for.

CBN, like CBD, is a cannabinoid related to THC. It's considered nonpsychoactive and is often used as a sleep aid. It is created through a chemical process of aging cannabis over a long period of time. I'm not sure CBN is as nonpsychoactive as people believe it is. Like CBD it calms the body down but when used in a blend, the inner visual experience of a journeyer has a greater sense of depth and richness. There's something more meaningful about the experience. In a sense, it feels like the experience goes deeper into the bones. It's possible that CBN isn't considered psychoactive simply because at higher doses, it really does put people to sleep. I tried a 5 mg patch of CBN before bed one evening just to try it out, and it was incredibly strong. I felt sedated for most of the next day. Strains with CBN are considered to be heavy, heavy indicas.

Another theory is that the sedative qualities of CBN allow for more THC to be consumed by the journeyer without the accompanying negative side effects of a heavy dose, like anxiety, nausea, and paranoia. I think both of these factors might be true. I've personally tried to take too much of a well-balanced Alchemy Blend just to test my upper limits, and it's very difficult to reach negative states of mind.

If it's true that the negative traits of certain strains are balanced out by positive traits of other strains, what would CBN feel like without the sleepiness? It seems to elicit a very evocative and very relaxed somatic experience. The psychedelic nature of the experience is paired with an incredible muscle relaxation that literally allows the body to tremble and shake away trauma and "stuckness." How do you balance the deep indica-like effects of a CBN strain? You pair it with the "tweakiest," most anxiety-provoking sativa you can find, a sativa most people avoid. What happens to this sativa when it's paired with a CBN indica? The anxiety disappears, but the mind remains alert and fully awake. And it just so happens that when paired, both types of strains, the tweaky sativa and the CBN indica, have significant closed-eye visuals and other psychedelic qualities. Sometimes it's like a VR excursion into the spirit world.

So that's the secret. It doesn't take much CBN to balance a strong sativa, usually about one-third to one-half of the indica third of the blend. I usually pair CBN indicas with lighter indicas that offer good body awareness without sedation to balance out the mixture. This is then paired with two or more sativas, with the most anxiety producing sativa taking up about one-third to one-half of the sativa in the blend (the same amount as the CBN strain). Combine these with equal parts hybrids—usually an indica-dominant hybrid, a true middle-of-the-road hybrid, and a sativa-dominant hybrid—and you might have a blend with an incredibly potent alchemy.

The name Alchemy Blend refers to a very specific union of opposites—what the psychologist Carl Jung would have called an "alchemical conjunction"—that manifests in blends that combine a deep CBN indica with a high sativa. These strains are not only dramatically opposite in their effects but in their ages as well. To make CBN, you have to let cannabis age. Young, fresh cannabis strains that have invigorating fragrances are the best sativas to pair with an old CBN strain. The pairing of the young with the old is one of the primary conjunctions in this work; the other primary conjunction is symbolized by the union of the masculine and the feminine. CBN doesn't come off of a freshly harvested plant. It can take many months to produce. Even as a sativa ages, it still becomes more CBN-dominant and less sativa, more indica. That's why its counterpart is the most freshly cut herb. A union of opposites: the new and the old, the king and the queen, the sativa and the indica.

I am still experimenting with the best way to make CBN, but so far what I've found to work the best is to place a high-THC indica strain into a large glass jar, cover it with a piece of cloth to create a shade, and let it sit in a window with indirect lighting. Every week, open the jar, smell it, let some new air in, and re-cover. Do this for many, many months. The shade prevents the flower from getting totally cooked by the sun. It can turn into a light greenish-yellow if that happens, and it's harsher to smoke. You could also try alternating between a dark closet and the sun or keep it in a dark closet for six months or more like my friends did. I don't generally have to worry about mold in Colorado because it's so dry here. But there might be specific requirements I don't know about to properly age cannabis in your location. I've talked to experts in the field about making CBN, and there doesn't seem to be much consensus. That said, these simple practices seem to work. As your cannabis ages, you will notice progress via the terpenes in the strain, which will begin to smell more sour. There's a loss of specific terpenes through this process, but the CBN is well worth it.

While the level 3 blend works really well, when I'm able to get a good CBN strain into the blend, I personally notice a significant difference. As you grow into this practice, find a good candidate for a CBN strain and purchase a quarter ounce or more of it. Place it in the jar and don't think about it too much. It'll start changing the effects of the strain after about a month, but older medicine is even better. As it ages, start working on level 1, level 2, and even level 3 strains. You might find certain combinations work really well for you.

Working with cannabis in this way is very meaningful, and it would be interesting to have someone scientifically explore the influence CBN has on psychedelic cannabis blends.

Dosage

Today's cannabis is often at least three times stronger than it was just twenty years ago, and it has a much wider range of effects. Based on potency alone, which may not accurately reflect the full experience of cannabis today, we can make some observations around the potency and dosage of a psychedelic cannabis experience. To preserve the terpene profiles, I only use raw flower, which isn't uniformly measurable. That said, it is possible to make some realistic assumptions about dosage.

A typical half-gram joint twenty years ago would have had a 5 to 10 percent THC concentration along with some CBD. Compare this to a half-gram joint today featuring a 20 to 30 percent THC potency and a guaranteed 0 percent CBD concentration. A 25 percent THC strain isn't uncommon. In milligrams, these numbers would equal 25 to 50 mg of THC in the joint from twenty years ago, and about 125 mg of THC in the typical joint today. In addition to being more than three times stronger, when we account for 0 percent CBD, as well as the greater terpene profile, the effects are also radically more complex. In my experience, the best psychedelic cannabis blends are within a 20 to 25 percent THC content range and have a very diverse terpene profile.

For example, a dose for someone who doesn't smoke cannabis regularly could be as little as one to two inhalations of the medicine. A typical pipe bowl of cannabis equates to about a third of a gram, and a single bowl is usually shared among several people. If you're sharing, for example, one-fourth of a third-gram bowl is about 20 mg of THC. This is about twice the typical dose of an edible sold in recreational cannabis shops, but some of this is also lost in the combustion of the material. Regardless, this dose would get most people who don't regularly smoke extremely high.

Based on the amount of cannabis still in the bowls after a Conscious Cannabis Circle, or after a psychedelic cannabis session, some people take only a few tokes (10 to 20 mg), while others consume half a bowl (30 to 40 mg) or the entire bowl or more (80 to 100 mg). Some participants consume twice this much. It just depends on their relationship and experience with the medicine. People regularly adjust their dosage—sometimes less, sometimes more—based on previous experiences. Because the terpenes balance themselves out, it's safer to take more of the medicine because of the reduced likelihood of panic and paranoia.

When smoked or vaped, it's possible to determine within the first five to ten minutes of a smaller dose whether it's safe for a journeyer to imbibe a significant amount more after that. The onset of the effects is quick, and paranoia and panic show up in the first few minutes more than 90 percent of the time.

The capacity to learn our own dose, based on our experience and the effect the medicine has on each of us, is a wonderful quality of psychedelic cannabis. After some practice, you'll be able to dial in to the exact state you're looking for. This practice is called subjective dosing and is very different from the standard dose recommendations of other psychedelics. We are all encouraged to take responsibility for our consumption, to listen to our inner guidance on how much to smoke, and to trust our previous experiences with the medicine.

As a guide, because I can't see someone's inner experience while they're lying there, I tell them before we begin that being sleepy or bored is a general indication they didn't get enough medicine, so they should sit back up and take more. Another indication of too low a dosage is the sensation of being almost where you want to be, but not quite. This awareness puts the responsibility of the intensity of the experience on the journeyer. I've learned to trust that people simply know best when to smoke more and when not to, cultivating a sense of agency, discernment, and ongoing consent.

How Much Do I Take?

A regular cannabis consumer can tolerate quite a bit of cannabis. A new user might only smoke once or twice before feeling strong effects. The key here, if these practices are new to you, is to start light, maybe even lighter than you think you should. I once worked with an elder who had never used cannabis but was trying it out because it was recommended to him for treating pain caused by cancer. He took a hit, nothing. Another hit, nothing. Then suddenly, he passed out. I caught him as he fell over and got him seated. His journey lasted several hours. I've caught other people on their way down as well, one of whom was a young man who wasn't new to cannabis at all. These things happen. Safety is important. If you're not sure, start slower than you think you should and stay seated until you know the effects of the medicine you've taken.

While a wide range of experiences occur, for most people, the psychedelic effects of this dosage last between an hour and fifteen minutes and an hour and a half. Longer, three-hour journeys typically have a short bathroom and smoke break in the middle.

Because onset is so quick and because cannabis gives us the capacity to pause an experience to take care of our body's needs, it's possible to very quickly reenter the full peak within a matter of minutes after the pause.

Testing a new cannabis blend is simple but creating the right blend is in itself its own journey. If choices are limited, say thank you, and go with what you have. It'll be good enough. If you find that you're bored or sleepy, again you might not have taken enough, or you might need to add more sativa to your blend. If you're anxious, add an indica, and try again. Depending on your tolerance, you may want to take what we call a "cannabis fast" for a few days, though doing so isn't always necessary.

Some people are very sensitive to cannabis, and others are more tolerant. Getting to know the dosage that works for your body and the strains that are the best for you is part of the learning process. Generally, I guide an intentional imbibing ceremony that includes as many as seven or more inhalations of the medicine in a short period of only five to ten minutes. With the right blends, this can induce a full psychedelic experience. For lighter, psycholytic or meditative experiences, half the inhalations is a good place to start. Listening to music, beginning with a gentle body scan (discussed in chapter 22), focusing on slow and rhythmic belly breathing, and relaxing into your body are all good and effective practices, which we will discuss in depth in part 4. It's a wonderful gift to our bodies and our souls to rest in the sacred space of this medicine.

12

A Revolutionary Application for CBD

One of the most interesting qualities of cannabis that make it radically different from other psychedelics is the fact that the plant offers in its own chemical makeup a natural antidote for difficult psychedelic experiences, including those induced by cannabis itself—namely, cannabidiol, or CBD. No other psychedelic medicine can make that claim. No one would recommend taking more LSD if you were having a bad trip, but you can take more of the right kind of cannabis to manage difficult experiences.

CBD is known to be a natural antianxiety, anti-inflammatory, and antipsychotic medication. It can relieve tension in the body, lower blood pressure, and return an elevated heart rate to a normal level. It basically calms down the nervous system.

While CBD is a great medicine to use in certain cannabis blends, in the main psychedelic blends I work with, I generally try to keep CBD out of the formulation except when there is a specific intention to address trauma symptoms. Because of its antipsychotic qualities, CBD may reduce the psychedelic nature of the experience. When CBD is used as an intervention in its water-soluble, or nano-encapsulated form, it can immediately resolve the negative side effects of THC during a difficult experience or help move us through a difficult experience with greater ease and physical comfort. It can reduce or eliminate a panic attack by lowering the heart rate, respiration rate, and blood pressure. This antidote can also significantly reduce the paranoia sometimes caused by psychedelics. Generally, a relatively low dose of 5 to 10 mg is more than enough to set any negative experience back onto a good path.

On the rare occasion a trip is difficult to manage, or you're excessively uncomfortable, ingesting nano-encapsulated tinctures of CBD (nano-CBD) or vaping pure CBD (without THC) almost immediately drops the experience to a physiologically safe and psychologically manageable level. This medicine should be in all of our psychedelic first aid kits as an important tool for psychedelic harm reduction. With this tool you should feel confident to explore the deepest psychedelic cannabis spaces.

Some people have asked me when one should take nano-CBD and when one should try to ride out the experience. Usually, some aspect of the experience is a little beyond manageable. It might be the speed of the inner vision, a discomfort in the body, a racing heart that just won't slow down even if you try breathing deeply, or breathing that is too shallow. From my experience, I've learned to trust my clients. I let them know a powerful adjunct and antidote is available should they want to try it. As an aspect of building agency into healing practices, learning how CBD affects your experience is an important part of the training.

I feel very strongly about the antidote potential of CBD. I personally think a nano-encapsulated CBD tincture or pure CBD vaporizer should be readily available as a harm reduction tool to every group using psychedelics. Not only does it reduce the negative experiences of psychedelic cannabis, it may also significantly reduce the negative experiences of other psychedelics, particularly those of extreme anxiety and panic. It is also very safe to use with other medicines. If you or a friend are having a difficult experience on another psychedelic medicine, like psilocybin or LSD, it is safe to take nano-CBD to help calm your anxiety and any discomfort in your body. The dose is going to be much higher than what's generally needed for a difficult psychedelic cannabis experience. If I were working in a psychedelic crisis situation, I would kindly offer a nano-CBD tincture, 5 to 10 mg sprayed under the tongue, every few minutes, coaching the person to slow their breathing and help them regulate their emotions and nervous system until they start to calm down. Nano-CBD takes more time to be effective with other psychedelics, but it is safe to take in large doses, and as needed. A primary concern for higher doses of CBD while in an altered state is lowering the blood-pressure a little too much, which is safe, but may lead to fainting. Please be mindful with your friends and your own safety. Take your time standing up and find your feet before walking.

PART THREE

Preparing for the
Psychedelic Cannabis
Experience

♦♦♦

There is a huge debate right now about mainstreaming psychedelics, making them safe, and keeping them contained, as though they were some sort of radioactive contagion. They're powerful tools, yes, but they don't deserve to be confined to the medical model or the clinical model or any model that places one human being between them and another human being, unjustified, as a gatekeeper, except truly to keep someone safe who is in legitimate need.

There is a lot of talk now about having guides and sitters with you in these medicine experiences. And there are real reasons for that, like stopping someone from hurting themselves accidentally or intentionally because of something revealed during this work. And I wholeheartedly agree with that. We clearly need more guides and sitters, and in the future, psychedelic therapy will be as common as psychotherapy and yoga. But not everyone has access to or can afford a trained guide or a sitter, particularly those who are struggling the most with trauma. What about them? Seriously—what about them? Are we ignoring them as a subtle system of control, to keep some sort of false status as gatekeepers to a fundamental human right? Who are we to demand that control, given the fundamental liberating nature of these experiences? Are we perhaps ignoring them because we're limited in our capacity to teach people to do the work safely on their own? If so, that's where this part of the book makes an effort to make a difference.

While there are still other gatekeepers like laws that prohibit most psychedelics, these are being systematically broken down. It is still going to take years, maybe even decades, to finally destroy these systems of control. What do we do in the meantime? Break the gate. We need access to these medicines now. Not ten years from now. To think otherwise is to wholly ignore the reality of climate crisis, the traumas of our current pandemic, the need for real social and economic justice reforms, and the extreme tragedies caused by racism and bigotry, just to name a few of the severe issues we face. These extreme problems, individually, feel nearly impossible to solve, but collectively feel nearly hopeless. This situation calls on us to address our trauma so we can be active participants in necessary, large-scale solutions right now.

This is where cannabis comes in. Cannabis is the first psychedelic to break free from the confines of not just the law in some places but even the clinical and medical models that limit and regulate psychedelic medicine use. Cannabis is paving the way for other psychedelic medicines in that it can be safely used by most people* as part of individual healing paths by those who do not have access to guides, sitters, and therapists.

The right to alter our own consciousness, something called cognitive liberty, is the most fundamental right we have. Without it, our First Amendment rights would be utterly meaningless. Yet this is the fight we're in right now. And it's not just a fight for our own consciousness; it's a fight over the right to have healthy and free bodies, as well. Having the right to heal your own trauma, on your own terms, is also fundamental.

It has been more than ten years now, but before I went back to graduate school to study psychedelics, my life had basically fallen apart. Those things sometimes happen, and it took me several years to regroup and get my feet stable beneath me again. During this time, I turned toward awareness of my body while using psychedelic medicines. Instead of going *out there* and escaping the limits of the body, even if for just a little while, I turned inward instead, and cast that whole light of awareness *into* my body. These were the most healing experiences I'd ever had.

---

*Cannabis may not be safe for everyone to do for a variety of reasons, such as a medical diagnosis, for example (see self-assessment in chapter 14).

I was working with some powerful substances, and I was always alone. I can't necessarily recommend the path I took to get to where I am now, but I can fundamentally say that these experiences helped make me who I am today. Since that time, I have learned from direct personal experience that having a guide is really wonderful and sometimes necessary. That said, guides are often not available when they're most required. And I can't ignore the fact that in some of my most profound healing experiences on psychedelics, I was completely and utterly alone in my process. Somehow the risk I took in being alone was a required part of the healing. There are some wounds too intimate to share even in skillfully held sacred spaces. I can't ignore this fact. And this is why I'm sharing the skills in this context now. If you find yourself alone, whether by necessity or by preference, this section is for you. But if you would prefer the presence of a trusted sitter, chapter 16 may be especially useful for you and the person you've chosen to witness your journey.

Learn to discern the difference between necessary and unnecessary risks and acknowledge that there's a huge gradient between the two. I advise reflecting on the self-assessment in chapter 14 prior to beginning your journey. Go slowly. Start lightly. Only do what you feel ready to do. Prepare for your experience and anticipate your needs before, during, and after the experience (see chapter 15). Set up a safe environment for the work (see chapter 17 for tips). Many journeyers enjoy working with music, and chapter 18 will assist you in deepening your practice with music. Finally, chapter 19 provides meditations to help connect you with the medicine and the experience. The healing will happen, and in the meantime, you're developing the skills and resiliencies to take full advantage of the healing experiences when they do happen. Whether going it alone, with a trusted sitter, or in a facilitated group experience, there's only one person who can take full responsibility for the outcome of your experience—you.

I would like to invite you to go with me into a deeper exploration of a primary purpose of this medicine: *healing your own trauma and uncovering your real potential.* I know that sounds somewhat New Agey, and I honestly hate that. But I'm not quite sure how else to say it. Working with psychedelic cannabis in this way has an incredible amount of meaning and depth. It can be archetypal and deeply symbolic, with profound releases through and out of the body. I have personally never experienced so much continual healing from any other practice. I see the changes in my clients all the time. Through a simple process, people can guide themselves and others to help the body and psyche release real trauma.

When trauma is released, a space is created that is naturally and organically filled with who we really are. We're just creating more space around us to grow into. It's as if a rock has been lifted off a smothered seed. It just knows to naturally grow. And now it can. Healing and waking up to the self seem to be the same process, and integration of the two is what we call living into our calling. It's just something that happens, because now it can.

Smoking psychedelic cannabis alone isn't what makes for therapeutic experiences. How you smoke it, in what context, and with what practices, greatly influences the states achieved. In the Medicinal Mindfulness terminology, we refer to these factors as set, setting, and skill. Since cannabis gives us agency in our psychedelic state, we have to continually choose to step into the process. Stepping into it repeatedly is like an epic journey of self-discovery. There are sometimes turbulent waters and uncertain opportunities, big emotions and complex fears. Navigating these inner terrains requires certain mindfulness practices, body postures, breath practices, and even a certain flow of music. It may sound complicated, but it's actually quite simple. I'd like to step into these practices with you now.

13

Learning to Set Sail

The practices and concepts discussed next are used to make cannabis a psychedelic, something a lot of people don't believe is possible, so these skill sets are extremely powerful tools and shouldn't be taken lightly. It is never appropriate to put yourself unnecessarily at risk to use psychedelic medicines. Doing so is an unskillful action, and it behooves us to do better if we can. This is the level of accountability required to work with psychedelics.

Our capacity to engage these practices as a skill set is developed over time and with practice. This isn't something you hear regularly regarding psychedelics, but it's very true. Healing trauma isn't something done to you or for you; it's a skill set that can be developed, practiced, and performed on your own like building a muscle by stretching and working out. And cannabis can be used regularly, even weekly or daily, allowing you to interact with these skill sets often to heal your trauma.

Another analogy I use for these practices is learning to sail. We have to learn the fundamental practices of sailing even before we get on a ship and then practice in a safe harbor before sailing by ourselves around the world. It just doesn't make sense to do otherwise, and people would rightly think we were crazy if we did. This is the same with psychedelics. The primary point of working with cannabis to heal trauma is being able to heal on our own terms. Smoking too much pot before you're ready is like putting a giant rocket booster on a little row boat. It might be quite the ride, and even fun, but the rocket isn't going to be that useful to you if it's beyond your capacity to engage the experience skillfully.

While you may be thinking, "It's just *pot*," it's extremely important not to underestimate the power of this medicine. I have been taken off guard by its potency a number of times. Also, I want to fully acknowledge that even though we're just using pot here, these skill sets translate very well to other psychedelic medicines. If these practices can render humble cannabis into a psychedelic, what would happen if they were used with traditional psychedelics? The answer is, quite a lot!

These practices are a skill set, and we're going to specifically discuss using them first to heal your own trauma and later to learn how to know yourself better and support what you want to do with your life. Mindful Journeywork, defined in my program as bringing mindfulness practices into psychedelic journey experiences to explore a particular intention, is a pretty simple practice, but it's extremely powerful and has many levels. I can't fit everything you'll encounter into one book, nor can I speak to what comes up in using these practices with other psychedelics. I'm only sharing what you need to get started; the medicine itself will be your primary teacher.

We will start with the psychedelic equivalents of strengthening exercises and other basic techniques. All I can say is that they are most important to our practice and what we'll fundamentally return to again and again, no matter how far along we are. These practices can be used at any stage of your healing process to continue the healing. And if healing is your primary intention, you may need no other psychedelic but cannabis.

14

Psychedelic Cannabis Safety Self-Assessment

A good case could be made that cannabis is one of the safest medicines available. That said, using cannabis does come with some risk, and it's not for everyone. Turning it into a psychedelic and using it solo also carries some inherent risks. As a psychedelic harm reduction model, Medicinal Mindfulness has developed several strategies to reduce that risk, and the first one is adequate self-assessment.

Another way to reduce risk is to work through these practices with a friend and agree to keep an eye out for each other based on these assessment criteria. If you're working solo, some of them may not apply to you. I'll speak more about working with a friend in chapter 16.

Starting on page 71, I've reproduced the safety self-assessment we use in our work to reduce risk and to assess what we need to watch for in every session. When it comes to safety, these decisions are not always black-and-white, but frankly, sometimes they are. And sometimes it's simply about creating a certain structure around the experience to reduce the likelihood of harm.

CANNABIS, PSYCHOSIS, AND MANIA

Cannabis can elicit a psychosis in people who already have a psychosis such as schizophrenia or are at a higher risk of having one. Cannabis can also trigger manic episodes in people who have bipolar disorder. Though some people do self-medicate with cannabis to help with manic symptoms, if you have these diagnoses, please be careful in your use with psychedelics and cannabis. You are strongly encouraged not to use psychedelics or to only use them under the recommendation of a trained professional. Don't smoke cannabis if it activates your symptoms and take CBD to support your stability and healing process. CBD is a powerful tool for helping heal and manage these sorts of symptoms.

SUICIDALITY AND SELF-HARM

Thoughts of suicidality and self-harm are indications that cannabis use may not be right for you. I have included hotline resources at the back of this book if you ever need to ask for help. Remember, you are not alone in your struggle, even if it feels that way. Psychedelics and cannabis are powerful tools and sometimes in working with them, we feel worse before we feel better. If your mental health stands right along these edges, please seek support. There are resources available to help you, even if they're not always perfect. Don't give up.

CANNABINOID HYPEREMESIS SYNDROME

Cannabinoid hyperemesis syndrome is a very uncommon reaction to cannabis that involves nausea, vomiting, and severe abdominal cramps. Doctors are still trying to figure it out. I've never personally experienced it with anyone, but doctors I know who work in emergency medicine and cannabis medicine have. Taking a hot shower can alleviate symptoms, but you will also want to go to a doctor. The primary recommendation is to quit using cannabis immediately, as this syndrome usually occurs in heavy, long-term users.

CANNABIS, THE LAW, AND YOUR PROFESSION

Cannabis is legal to possess and use in many places in the United States, but the laws are complex and rapidly evolving. A terrible consequence of using cannabis in places where it's still illegal to possess the medicine is the possibility of arrest, and I really can't advise you to take that risk. If cannabis is illegal in your area, all of these practices can be facilitated with a powerful breathwork practice that I also describe how to use here. If you're still curious about using cannabis, consider joining the legalization movement. There's bound to be one in your area. You can also consider relocation or travel. I know a very large number of people who have moved to places where cannabis is legal, either to help themselves, a loved one, or a child to heal. This is totally acceptable, in my opinion. From a harm reduction perspective, sometimes it's safer to break the law to heal than to live with trauma, but more and more legal avenues exist these days. Don't take unnecessary risks.

OTHER CONTRAINDICATIONS: REASONS NOT TO USE PSYCHEDELICS AND PSYCHEDELIC CANNABIS

This discussion shouldn't be considered an exhaustive list. As I've said, the primary way to stay safe with cannabis is to start lighter than you think you should. Psychedelic cannabis experiences are very safe, but they're not for everyone.

While there's significant scientific evidence that supports the skillful and intentional use of cannabis to alleviate or significantly reduce the symptoms of physical and psychological disorders, people with serious mental health disorders sometimes use psychedelics and cannabis with the unrealistic expectation that these experiences alone will cure them. Often people misunderstand the necessity for additional support or treatments when working with serious concerns. Unstable interpersonal relationships and a history of various treatments can be additional factors indicating increased risk.

These practices shouldn't be a substitute for medical or psychiatric treatment if it's accessible, and we don't recommend them for people with serious psychiatric disorders or physical conditions that may impair their ability to do these practices safely.

PSYCHEDELIC CANNABIS SAFETY SELF-ASSESSMENT

Psychedelic cannabis experiences are far more closely akin to other psychedelic experiences than guided meditation or traditional psychotherapy sessions. Taking this self-assessment is strongly recommended before using psychedelic cannabis. Answering a yes to any of the safety self-assessment questions below may indicate a need to slow down and check in with a friend or other ally before proceeding. Some of them indicate stronger concerns than others and might even require discontinuing the use of cannabis altogether and replacing it with breathwork or CBD only, if it's a significant concern.

Notes and recommendations on how to assess an answer are included below each question. Truthfully answering "no" to every question doesn't always guarantee a positive experience. By doing this work, you're agreeing to take full responsibility for any outcome you might experience.

Again, psychedelic cannabis is very safe, but it's not for everyone. Please be honest with yourself regarding your readiness for exploring psychedelic medicines.

1. **Are you pregnant or nursing?** The decision to take any psychedelic, including cannabis, should be considered carefully if you are pregnant or nursing. Any medical professional would strongly recommend against it.

2. **Do you have any past or present medical conditions (either physical or mental) that may affect your ability to safely participate in this event?** A psychedelic cannabis experience isn't appropriate for persons with cardiovascular problems, severe hypertension, severe mental illness, recent surgery or fractures, acute infectious illness, or epilepsy, without significant supervision.

3. **Have you ever required significant treatment or been hospitalized for a psychological or emotional disorder or for any other psychological or emotional reason?** Mental health contraindications (reasons not to work with psychedelics) include, but aren't limited to, clinically significant acute anxiety or other severe mood disorders, psychosis, bipolar disorders, personality disorders, acute/unprocessed trauma and PTSD (without support), acute addictions, suicidal ideation/instances of or desire to self-harm, and tendencies for disruptive behavior. The key words here are "significant treatment." While psychedelics can help heal many of the concerns associated with these diagnoses, it's imperative you have adequate support. If you're not sure, seek guidance from a trained professional. Another way to take care of yourself is to start extremely light with the medicine.

4. **Have you ever had a severe, adverse reaction to using cannabis or other psychedelic medicines—physically, emotionally, or otherwise?** Again, start with a very low dose and go slowly. You may have simply taken too much or taken it in the wrong context. Have a friend with you for support, if you can.

5. **Has a health professional ever advised you to cease or otherwise limit consumption of cannabis, psychedelic medicines, or altered states practices? Why?** Be honest with yourself here. Did they have a point, or were they just part of the antidrug group?

6. **Have you ever experienced extreme paranoia or anxiety, panic attacks, or other profoundly negative experiences while using cannabis or any psychedelic drug or during any other times in your life, that required a significant intervention?** We've

all experienced anxiety in one form or another; the key here is did your episode require a significant intervention, or were you actually visibly shaky in the moments before imbibing the medicine? It may simply be too much for you at this time, so consider doing all of these practices completely sober first. These are some of the most common, but still very uncommon, side effects of working with cannabis (and they're addressed in more detail in chapter 25). The fact is, though, you wouldn't be doing this work if you weren't struggling in some way. These risks are manageable with the right practices.

Also, if you're prone to anxiety, panic, or paranoia, you should purchase some nano-encapsulated, pure CBD (no THC) tincture before you get started. It's an incredible tool that can drop all of these symptoms to manageable levels.

7. **Have you ever fainted, blacked out, or otherwise adversely lost consciousness while on cannabis or any psychedelic medicine?** While this can happen to anyone, some are more susceptible than others, particularly those with low blood pressure. This is one of the ways you can seriously hurt yourself. Remember, CBD can lower blood pressure, as well, so it's important to take your time when you stand up after these experiences or when you use the restroom. You can fall over and hurt yourself. If you're dizzy or light-headed after your experience, it most likely means you need more time, and you aren't back yet. Stay seated! And again, take your time when you stand up.

8. **Have you ever dealt with a pattern of unstable relationships that caused you significant distress?** Psychedelics disrupt established patterns we want to change, but sometimes if we're in a relational space that is already unstable, they may make the patterns worse before they get better. Unstable relationships are sometimes an indicator of a need to slow down transformational work and a need to seek professional therapeutic support to help stabilize your life before continuing.

9. **Have you ever had extremely unusual or disconcerting thoughts or ideas, or extreme levels of energy (inability to sleep for days or racing thoughts, or alternatively, extremely low energy) after the effects of a psychedelic or cannabis should have worn off?**

10. **Have you ever seen or heard things or people that weren't there after the effects of a psychedelic or cannabis should have worn off?**

11. **Have you ever obsessed over an idea or belief in a way that has caused difficulties in your life?**

Questions 9 through 11 are pointing to very serious symptoms and might be an indication of a mild to severe manic or psychotic episode. This is where we ask friends and family for support in our healing process, especially if we're prone to these things. Trauma injures our psyches, and these injuries can sometimes show up in this way. Don't go it alone. These symptoms are the hardest to be aware of. If you're concerned about yourself, a friend, or a family member, seek professional help or call the hotlines listed at the back of the book.

12. **Do you have any acute, current, or past substance abuse or addiction concerns?** People are successfully using cannabis and CBD to reduce their dependence on opiates and pain medication, as well as to reduce the severe withdrawal symptoms of getting off of other drugs and alcohol. There's significant evidence to support this. Also, substance use and abuse and trauma go hand in hand. While cannabis can be used to treat addiction, addiction treatment often requires additional support. Please get some help or at the very least attend self-help groups. Some are listed at the back of this book. You don't have to go it alone.

13. **Are you currently on any medications, supplements, or recreational drugs that could affect you and keep you from safely participating in a psychedelic cannabis experience?** Again, these are extremely powerful tools, and psychedelic cannabis is a powerful

medicine. Using it in conjunction with other medicines, psychedelic or otherwise, increases risk. Cannabis is generally the safest medicine to take with other prescriptions, psychoactive or otherwise, and is also used as a tool to wean off of SSRIs (selective serotonin reuptake inhibitors) and other medications, but this often requires clinical or medical support.

14. **Do you or anyone in your circle have a history of disruptive or violent physical, sexual, or emotional behavior?** This is more for when you're doing this work with another person. Are you safe, and are they safe? Disruptive behavior includes rage and arguing over little things, threatening to injure yourself or another, or using psychedelics in ways that are emotionally or sexually manipulative. Working with friends and in groups requires consensual agreements so these behaviors are nowhere near appropriate in psychedelic states. Please seek support in your healing process.

    Disruptive behavior doesn't include spontaneous healing and transformational releases that require a long unwinding. The best way to keep yourself physically safe from big physical releases is to have a lot of space around you in the experience.

15. **Do you have a history of traumatic or difficult life events that hasn't been addressed or isn't being supported therapeutically?** Psychedelic cannabis experiences are best used to complement psychotherapy, not replace it. Not everyone has the resources to work with a psychotherapist, but many of us do. There are social services available, as well as student practitioners, in all therapy programs.

    Having difficult past experiences unexpectedly come up in a psychedelic cannabis experience is somewhat the point. It's one of the ways we clear unprocessed trauma. But it can be too much at times, and if that happens, turn toward resourcing and self-care. Let your body and mind catch up to the healing process. If you're ever uncertain of your safety, immediately seek professional help. Asking for help is the greatest gift you can give yourself and your family.

16. **Do you have any present concerns regarding suicide or self-harm?** While there are different degrees of suicidality, any concern about hurting yourself is serious. You might just have a wish, or you might be actively cutting. Either way, please know you're not alone. Help is available.

    Working with a close friend will be an important way to keep yourself safe. Making agreements about self-care will keep you well-resourced as you work with difficult material. Sometimes it does feel worse before it gets better, but that's actually a significant sign of progress. It means the wound is halfway out. And never forget that you can heal on terms that work for you.

    If you or someone you know is in immediate risk of hurting yourself or another, please call 911 immediately.

17. **As you contemplate a psychedelic cannabis experience, or when checking in with yourself right before it begins, are you extremely anxious?** While mild to moderate anxiety is completely normal before a psychedelic cannabis experience, extreme anxiety, panic, and physically shaking or trembling before an experience is an indication to pause and check in with yourself before beginning. It may be that you're already in the experience and doing these practices without cannabis might be enough. You might also want to try working with CBD alone, or taking CBD before the blend to see if it settles you down.

    If severe anxiety is one of the symptoms you're wanting to treat with psychedelic cannabis, you might want to increase the indica and CBN strains in the mix or even add a CBD strain. Avoid the most extreme sativas.

18. **Have you recently had a major transformational experience, with a psychedelic medicine or otherwise, that feels almost complete but not quite, or unresolved?** I think this is one of the most interesting phenomena I've experienced. Those with strong meditation practices, or those who have done a lot of transformational work, with or without psychedelics, appear to have a higher

chance of immediately going into full, psychedelic breakthrough experiences using psychedelic cannabis. It's almost as if they're already primed, and the cannabis helps complete the remaining 10 percent of the work to do. This is good news, but these experiences can be intense. Work only in a safe and prepared space in case this happens. You might end up rolling all over the floor and such.

19. **Do you ever feel extremely uncomfortable in group transformational processes?** This question is indicative of another symptom of trauma. It's hard to be vulnerable in groups because the nervous system is amped up, and there's a feeling of a lack of safety. These practices render the practitioner vulnerable, typically lying on your back with eye coverings on. This may even be one of the primary reasons you're choosing to do the work on your own right now, and I completely relate to that. Go for it.

    That said, being in a community is also part of the healing, so when you're ready, even if you feel a little uneasy, start developing friendships around this work. See chapter 16 on working with another person.

20. **Are you currently involved in any legal proceedings? Criminal or civil?** Does your job test for drugs? Because of the controversial nature of cannabis, I can't guarantee working with cannabis is always safe to do, even where it's legal. Testing positive for it in a drug screening can cause problems with probation, can stop you from getting a job, and can get you fired, even if you've never used cannabis on the job. The court system is no joke, and I recommend you do what it takes to stay out of it or get out of it as quickly as you can. Smoking pot isn't worth these risks. Consider breathwork practices instead (see chapter 23).

21. **Are you currently employed, a student, or otherwise financially stable?** Financial stability can mean a lot of different things to different people but what I am pointing to here is the need to have some financial security in your life to safely engage psychedelic

practices. If you're struggling with food scarcity, it may be more important to address that first before working with these practices.

22. **Do you have a safe home environment and a stable residence?** Again, if you don't feel safe in your own home, or you are homeless or approaching homelessness, it is important that these conditions are addressed first before engaging in these practices. If you live with someone who is abusive toward you, please seek professional support or call the hotlines listed at the back of the book.

23. **Anything else you think might be a factor?** Normally this is something we'd go over in a session before we begin, but take some time to explore this question. Often a concern isn't a firm no, but it might be a not yet. Take your time and write down anything that comes up for you. This is something that would be great to journal about. What are your deepest concerns? What are your greatest hopes? Start bringing those into the light of attention so you can do something about them. Again, this is healing on your terms.

Most of these risks can be easily managed by going at a pace and a medicine dosage that work best for you.

Preparation
and Integration

During a psychedelic cannabis experience, you are likely to experience increased heart rate and a heightened awareness of physical sensations, as well as trembling or shaking as trauma discharges from the nervous system. This is normal and nothing to be afraid of. The session may be very visual/imaginal, verbal/relational, or subtle/energetic. Some clients talk the whole time, while others are mostly silent. The most important thing for you to know is that your senses, inner awareness, and emotions will be heightened and that by breathing and self-regulating through this experience, you'll be able to turn toward deep material within yourself for healing.

Describing the intensity and implications of the experience is difficult. While sometimes healing feels good and brings relief, sometimes progress doesn't feel this way. Sometimes, it's extremely difficult. For example, having to work through a memory you didn't know was there about something that happened or realizing something difficult about yourself you don't like admitting. Sometimes even positive realizations are difficult because they require reorienting our entire way of living.

While I normally recommend seeking counseling as part of your healing support network, counseling isn't always as accessible as we would like it to be. Again, there may be other resources in your area that are more affordable. These include integration groups as well as psychedelic societies and clubs. Creating the right supportive environment for your healing process is like having an insurance policy on your transformation. Sometimes it can catch you before you fall too hard into something avoidable.

Take an inventory of all interpersonal and intrapersonal resources available to you. By bringing awareness to your support system, and by noticing what happens in your body as you register these resources, you will naturally relax and be better prepared for psychedelic work. These resource lists can also be compiled into a collage or mandala form.

Start by creating a list with three sections labeled *internal, external, and transpersonal resources* as follows:

- **Internal resources**—Things about yourself that help you cope, such as a healthy self-esteem, a sense of humor, a sense of purpose
- **External resources**—People or things in your support system, such as close friends and family, communities you're a part of, favorite nature trails, pets, and so on
- **Transpersonal resources**—That which is sacred to you and/or offers you hope and support, including the Divine, the Mystery, Mother Nature, the Unseen World, God, and so on. These resources can be imaginal or energetic, spiritual or archetypal in nature and may include ritual, ceremony, prayer, and meditation. For example, the Goddess, Hanuman, ancestors, or animal spirits.

Use these lists of resources as a blueprint for your network of support. Map it out and write down specific names and phone numbers. Start making connections and speaking to allies about your intentions. You don't have to tell everyone what you're doing, just the key people you know and love and who support you.

As you're developing your network, it's probably also time to start thinking a little more about self-care. Self-care is essential during every stage of your transformational cannabis journey (before, during, and after). You're choosing to enter into the unknown, which can make you feel vulnerable and excited at the same time. You will need to be as resourced and as regulated as possible because your overall stress level will impact both your inner experience and your capacity for getting as much out of the experience as possible. This isn't to say you shouldn't journey if you've had a stressful day; it just means that overall self-care is going to have an ongoing impact on your practice.

Simply put, it is safer to do psychedelic healing practices if you have a solid network of resources and a healthy regimen of self-care, obviously, but our expectations and needs are not always met, let alone fully realized in our lives. This is the whole point of our desire. There's something inherently incomplete in or missing from our lives that drives us to this work. So instead, think of your resources and self-care as an orientation, like a destination on a map, and simply start moving toward it with concrete steps. For example, say you want to run five miles three times a week. It's okay to start out with a nice, brisk walk.

Don't let feelings of lack limit you. After all, this is what we're working to heal. But also pay attention to serious holes in your resources and self-care regimen because these are the things that make psychedelic medicines unsafe.

Here are some self-care practices you can do before a psychedelic experience.

Before the Experience

- In preparation for a cannabis session, try to get plenty of rest, eat clean and healthy foods, and stay hydrated.
- Do your best to avoid overworking the day before.
- Avoid substances or activities harmful or distracting to your growth work.
- Consider meeting with a medicine-friendly therapist or mentor or join a community integration circle for additional support and inspiration on your medicine path.
- Do some journaling and write out your intentions for the cannabis session.

- Set up your space so it feels nourishing to each of your senses. Use soft blankets, beautiful music, refreshing smells (essential oils, for example), and delicious snacks in a clean room. Consider having something beautiful as a focal point, such as an altar or vase of flowers.
- Spend quiet, reflective time in nature, if possible.
- Meditate.
- Dress comfortably in loose clothing, stretch out, and eat before starting a session.
- Most importantly, find or create a mindfulness practice that works for you. It could be yoga, hiking, meditation, prayer, art, music, cooking, or anything else that relaxes you, stills your busy mind, and encourages inner listening. Having an ongoing mindfulness practice is the single most important building block for effective psychedelic cannabis work.

Self-care doesn't just happen before and after a session. Particularly in psychedelic sessions that will last many hours, we're required to keep refilling our cup throughout the experience. The work simply isn't sustainable without self-care. Here are some ways to take care of yourself during sessions.

During the Experience

- Eat, drink, move, and stretch as needed while also maintaining enough stillness to keep your focus turned inward.
- Continually bring your awareness into what's happening in your body. Which parts of your body feel relaxed and open? Where do you feel tension or pain? Breathe slowly and deeply into the belly, then completely let it go. Repeat.
- Do what works for you to stay in your body (breathing deeply, tapping, adjusting your posture, finding a place in the body that feels good and savoring the sensations there, using essential oils, holding a grounding stone or crystal, burning sage). Choose

cannabis strains that increase body awareness and sensation so you don't stay in your head the whole time.

- Call in your transpersonal resources (a.k.a. guides, ancestors, saints, God, the Divine, Mother Nature, and so on). Consider placing symbols of this sacred support system on your altar.

We use a Buddhist saying about enlightenment as a post-psychedelic journey integration practice: "Before Enlightenment, chop wood, carry water. After Enlightenment, chop wood, carry water." Take time to take care of your life and make it healthy and sustainable. I personally like to do housework and simple chores. They're a great way to stay active, and something about the physical activity supports the integration process. In a sense, I still feel productive while letting my mind and my psyche rest. Somehow, through this process, I gain greater understanding of my experience. Here are some other suggestions for self-care after a journey experience.

After the Experience

- Get out in nature and breathe deeply.
- Move your body; you've been still for a long time.
- Journal or make art or music about your cannabis experience.
- Take a hot bath with Epsom salts and lavender.
- Meet with a trusted friend, mentor, or therapist (you'll need a safe place to tell your story in confidentiality).
- Nourish your five senses.
- Take time to meditate and contemplate what came up for you during the session.
- Reach out to the people who care about you, support this process, and can help you integrate.
- Attend a community integration circle, or if there isn't one in your area, start one.
- Get plenty of rest.

ONGOING INTEGRATION

Most people think the peaks of the psychedelic state are the final destination, when in fact, the peak is more of the midway point to an even higher destination. This most important step involves integrating your experience into your life and facilitating lasting change. Yes, a few hours of enlightenment is really nice, but it's only so useful if it doesn't support the long-term healing of post-traumatic stress.

These self-care practices, used in conjunction with the psychedelic cannabis experiences, are healing in and of themselves, and the outcome should move you toward a sense of healing and relief over time. That said, symptom management isn't really the only or even the highest form of healing. Stepping into who we truly are and expressing ourselves in this world might be closer to the truth here. This requires real and intentional integration.

Healing is a process that requires much reflection. What did you learn? What do you understand that you didn't before? Go and test it out in the real world. How did it make a difference in your life? How was it successful? How was it not? What happened? Try again. Step back into the psychedelic experience space. Clear more trauma. What else did you learn? What else did you discover? How does this new understanding impact what you're implementing in your life? Go give it a try. What did you learn? Above all else, keep going as if healing were inevitable (because it is).

The healing and awakening processes associated with psychedelic cannabis happen in steps and stages and then, all of the sudden, there's an unexpected release into a new way of being. We don't have to try to make it happen; it happens naturally through sustained effort.

Psychedelic overvisioning is attempting to integrate too many psychedelic-inspired ideas at once. It's a common mistake to underestimate the work involved in big projects when solutions were so clearly apparent in their complete form in a psychedelic state. Bring the big ideas down to the real-world level. Maybe the inspiring idea is a symbol to strive for in ways a bit closer to home. At the very least, just try the next step, and if that's too big, explore intermediate steps to break it down. A healing process that only matters to you, matters enough. Take your time and give yourself permission to enjoy the process.

CANNABIS FASTS

While there are plenty of legitimate reasons to take cannabis daily, for example, helping with medical diagnoses or finding relief from severe pain, for some people, a cannabis fast is a very meaningful experience. A cannabis fast simply means taking a break from using cannabis. This can range in duration from a few days before an intentional experience, to a week, a month, or even more. Fasts give the cannabis receptors in your brain a chance to clear up a bit, so the next intentional experience can be stronger. While it's not necessary to take a fast before a psychedelic cannabis session, if you are frustrated with your results or are unable to reach psychedelic states with your blend, you may want to consider taking a cannabis fast and then breaking the fast in an intentional session. Sometimes fasting can create extreme psychedelic experiences.

INTENTION SETTING, INTEGRATION QUESTIONS, AND WRITING PROMPTS

Journaling during the week before and the week after a session is a great way to help process the work. Listed below are the questions and writing prompts we use to prepare for and help us integrate our own and our clients' experiences.

Preparation Questions
- What are my goals? What do I hope to receive from this session?
- What fears or concerns do I have about this work, if any?
- What am I willing to check at the door before entering into this work?

- Do I believe in miracles? Is there a part of me open to this being easy?
- What critical or judgmental voices might show up that could distract me from deepening my process, trusting the medicine, or getting the most out of the day?
- What are my personal resources? Who can I speak to or pretend to write to in a journal about this experience?
- Are there any objects I'd like to bring in with me to place on the altar during the ceremony?

Intention-Setting Prompts

- Something that is very present for me right now is . . .
- Something I'm avoiding is . . .
- I have concerns about . . .
- I'm curious about . . .
- I'm inspired to explore . . .
- I'm ready to let go of . . .
- In this moment, I deeply desire and long for . . .

Once you journal for a while answering these questions or working with the prompts, there may be certain themes that emerge. Circle them and organize them. Get to know them. After that, you can write a summary of your intentions, called an intention statement. Ways to start an intention statement include the following:

- Thank you for giving me this opportunity to . . .
- I'm choosing to . . .
- My intention is . . .

Integration Support Questions

- Who in my life can support me after this experience?
- Who is a safe person to share my experience with, or who can support me in my unfolding?

- Are there any people who aren't safe to discuss this with? Why?
- What's possible now that wasn't possible before?
- Do I feel safe? (If not, please seek professional help.)

Integration Prompts
- What touched me the most was . . .
- What feels different now is . . .
- What I realized was . . .
- Something beautiful I remember about my experience is . . .
- When I felt stuck or challenged . . .
- What I learned or remembered about myself was . . .
- My body . . .
- My soul . . .
- What I know to be true about what happened is . . .
- After this journey, I feel inspired to . . .

Again, once you journal for a while answering these questions or working with the prompts, as with intentions, integration themes might emerge. Circle them and organize them. Get to know them. After that, you can write a summary of your intentions regarding integration, what you want to bring into your life or step into. This is called an integration statement. Ways to start an integration statement include the following:

- I commit to . . .
- I'm inspired to . . .
- I'm choosing now to . . .

Integration practices are imbedded throughout this book. There are additional resources for integration on our Medicinal Mindfulness website, including *The Medicinal Mindfulness Psychedelic Integration Guidebook*.

16

Psychedelic Cannabis Peer-Sitting

While it is generally safer to work with someone than alone, not all of us have that opportunity, at least in the beginning. Those of you who do are very fortunate. Take a risk and share your interest in this work with someone you know and trust. See what they say. They might bring up questions or concerns you hadn't considered, or they might be interested in the practices, too. Working with someone collaboratively in this way is called peer-sitting. Peer-sitting is simply taking turns staying sober to keep a gentle eye on the one going through the journey. Journeying with each other, as an alternative to peer-sitting, is taking the medicine together and remaining in your own, internal experience, and not taking turns sitting for each other. Both are possible to engage safely with cannabis. It might be that some friends or small groups start peer-sitting for each other, taking turns to journey, but then become skillful enough working with cannabis that everyone feels comfortable journeying together without a sober sitter.

I have a whole training program on how to become what is called a cannabis-assisted psychedelic sitter, guide, and therapist. It's a detailed process and offers many techniques. The role of a peer-sitter is to simply keep an eye on the journeyer to make sure they remain safe while staying completely hands-off physically and energetically unless they have to support the journeyer. A peer-sitter might also be in charge of the music, remind the journeyer to take CBD if the experience feels too out of control, and may gently offer some snacks afterward. Sitters are there to fully support and be of service to the journeyer. It is not the job of the journeyer to take care of the sitter in these spaces.

It is an incredibly vulnerable position to take psychedelic medicines and lie down with an eye covering on next to someone sitting for you, especially if you're doing this work for healing. It's important you know and trust the person you choose to work with. This could be a best friend, family member, or life partner. Even with this trust, it's appropriate to have a conversation to make specific agreements around expectations, including safety, touch, and other issues. I have included the Medicinal Mindfulness Psychedelic Experience Agreement in the next section as a model for this discussion.

Everyone involved in an experience should also review the safety self-assessment in chapter 14 and be ready to stay grounded if someone has a big experience. As mentioned, shaking and unusual movements during these sessions are not uncommon and as long as the journeyer is not close to something that could cause injury, nonintervention is the course of action we recommend. These practices are about developing a trust in our body, its intelligence, and its ability to turn naturally toward healing.

As a peer-sitter, it's important not to glare at the person on the journey. Instead we recommend keeping "half an eye" on the journeyer and the remainder of your focus on your own experience. I usually sit parallel to my clients, so I also remain energetically neutral. Your sole job is to keep your friend safe.

If the journeyer asks for help, usually hand-holding and reassuring words are enough. If the experience still feels too difficult, offer CBD. I've learned to trust the resiliency of the human spirit.

Afterward, your peer-sitter is your primary resource for helping you integrate your experience. You might set up agreements to be in touch after the experience, checking in over the phone or over a cup of tea. Sharing your memories of an experience with an understanding friend is a wonderful way to help you integrate. Peer-sitters should take notes of things you speak about to help you remember key moments.

Once you have fully completed your experience, you will have the opportunity to be a peer-sitter for your friend. Remember, it is okay to go it alone if you're called to, or if you're isolated where you live. Working intentionally with psychedelic cannabis is often one of the first steps in breaking us out of our isolation.

PSYCHEDELIC EXPERIENCE AGREEMENT FOR PEER SITTING

As representatives of the psychedelic community we choose to exemplify safe psychedelic experiences. Safety allows for depth, healing, and awakening and is a universal right for all people in psychedelic spaces. The purpose of this agreement is to clarify expectations and appropriate behavior before we have a psychedelic experience together and to help elicit the safest spaces we can create for psychedelic healing purposes.

1. We affirm that this agreement can only be made in a sober state, and we agree that once any medicine is taken, even if the medicine hasn't activated yet, we will not change the agreement until we are sober again, even if we all agree we want to. We agree to not break or change this agreement even if God/the Divine/the Universe/ Truth tells us directly and without a doubt to change it or break it.
2. Above all, we agree to respect each other's boundaries, treat each other with respect, and to keep each other safe.
3. Before we begin, we agree to complete a simple safety assessment, to be truthful about and discuss our current psychological state and life circumstances. We affirm that we are ready for the experience we're choosing to have.
4. We agree to have a conversation around consensual touch before the medicine is taken. Touch is always consensual. Consent about some-

thing not discussed cannot be given after a medicine is imbibed. Permission is always requested and affirmed before touching. We agree that touch is never sexual in nature in a psychedelic therapy session.

5. We agree to be mindful of externalizing our inner experiences and to be aware of our projections and transference (both positive and negative) that we may place on the experience, the facilitator, or the medicine. We agree to discuss our perceptions and to check in around feelings of safety or lack of safety if we become anxious or paranoid.

6. We agree to keep confidentiality and not share details of our experience with others except in situations that require significant intervention to prevent harm or where reporting is legally mandated, such as child or elder abuse, suicidality, or self-harm.

7. We agree to have back-up support in the form of a trusted emergency contact and to share the contact information with the facilitator or group. We agree to seek immediate professional support for any significant medical or mental health emergency.

8. We agree to only work with clean medicine that is tested, accurately measured, and responsibly sourced. We agree to be educated about the medicines we use and their legality.

9. We agree to only use medicines that we know are personally safe for us to use physically, mentally, psychologically, and spiritually.

10. We agree to designate a specific location that represents the boundaries of the experience and to not leave the confines of this safe space until the completion of the experience. We agree to not bring into or do anything dangerous or harmful in the psychedelic experience space.

11. We agree that anyone imbibing a medicine will not drive until the following day and until it is safe to do so.

12. We agree to speak at least once before the psychedelic experience for intention setting, safety assessments, and preparation support and at least once after the experience for a safety check-in and integration

support. If this is part of a professional service, the full cost of the entire protocol is outlined before we begin.

13. As the sitter/guide/therapist of the experience I agree to share my training and expertise verbally or through a disclosure statement and that I affirm to have adequate supervision support, training, and experience to facilitate the experience we are having safely. My fees are clearly outlined, will not change, and are in alignment with my skill, training, experience, and to similar services within my locale. I agree to only work within my scope of training and expertise, such as only doing body work if I am trained to do so or only working with specific clinical concerns (e.g., trauma, PTSD, and other significant mental health issues) if I am trained to do so. Thank you and safe travels! Many blessings to you on this sacred journey of healing and discovery.

Number 13 is specifically for working with a professional guide and is strongly recommended. Psychedelic therapy is an emerging field, and many people claim to be guides without adequate training. Ask questions about their training and experience. Any guide would agree to these thirteen criteria at a minimum if they have an ethical and skillful practice.

Take responsibility for your experiences and make them work for you within your own constraints and needs. No one has the right to put you into a position that feels unsafe for their own healing. If you don't feel safe, walk away before you even get started. In the end, this is just cannabis, so even if you have smoked, call a cab and get out of the situation. Having these agreements allows everyone to stay with difficult experiences, even paranoia, for healing purposes.

17

The Healing Space

Creating the space for these experiences can be a lot of fun and a meaningful experience on its own. Many of my students send me pictures of their setups, either a spare bedroom made into a meditation space, a temporary space in their living room, or on their bed if they have to. I am very fortunate to have a private meditation studio with plenty of room, but this wasn't always the case. I still use the same meditation altar I built in graduate school. The altar is simple, about four feet across, with shelves above an open area. I used to have it right beside my bed in an area a little bit wider than a yoga mat. I've also graduated from simple computer audio to a surround-sound speaker system with strong subwoofers and a lot of power. As your life and your intentions for your journey change, your space may change as well. Most importantly, make the space you have work for you, no matter what.

The first key to creating a healing space is safety. Don't take chances. If there's something in the space you can stumble on, do something about it. Pay attention to hard edges near where you will be lying down. Do you have enough room to stretch, roll, or move if you have to? Can you fall off of something? If your only space is your bed, it might be safer to put the mattress on the floor. If you're using candles, always put them in a container and keep them away from where you will be lying.

The second key to a healing space is privacy. It's important you're not disturbed in your experience. If you have roommates, let them know what you're doing and try to schedule your session when no one is home.

If you're working with a peer-sitter, set up a protocol of what to do if there's a knock on the door. It isn't that common, but it does happen. Ignore it. That package delivery can wait. But most importantly, these are meant to be private experiences where you can cry, sing, scream, or laugh if you want.

Remember that everything will be amplified, including the symbolic meanings of things. Therefore, take out the trash, do your dishes and laundry, and get rid of any old, moldy food in the fridge. Before enlightenment, chop wood, carry water. Is there anything left unsaid between you and your partner or roommate? Relationally, is there any trash that needs to be taken out before you begin your journey? Below is a list of other elements to consider as you ready your space for journeying.

- Open doors and windows to air out the space.
- Vacuum, dust, and clear the clutter.
- Note where the speakers are in relation to your neighbor's walls. Also, if you want to make noise, is it a safe place to do that?
- Soften the lights by using small lamps, candles, and/or dimmer switches.
- Plan for comfort: ready pillows, blankets, padding, eye coverings, and/or earphones.
- Consider using incense or sage to cleanse the room with pleasant fragrances.
- Consider using sweetgrass or other herbs to call in and invite that which you would like to cultivate in ceremony.
- Think about how each of your senses—touch, taste, smell, sight, hearing—experiences your sacred space. For example, if you're preparing the perfect sacred space for your nose, what scents are or aren't present? If you're preparing the perfect sacred space for your ears, what sounds are or aren't present? And so on.
- What images, statues, or other visuals are sacred to you? For example, a bowl of fall leaves from your morning walk, a Ganesh sculpture, a photograph of your grandmother, a tarot spread.

Physical objects help us make things real and hold the ineffable in our physical realities. What physical objects and images have meaning for you? Surround yourself with them. Make this space all about you. Make it look like the inside of your soul.

- Use tapestries to cover the TV or other screens or any other energies that aren't invited into your space. Start collecting tapestries or fabrics you love.

You will most likely be working on the floor. Beds are nice but are sometimes a little too comfortable. I generally use thin futons or other mats. Yoga mats are perfectly fine, as well. Be sure to create a very comfortable setting with extra pillows and blankets and a bolster for under your knees, especially if you have lower back pain. Create an eye covering with soft fabric, as well, or use a blindfold for sleeping. For sitting up during parts of your journeywork, you might want a meditation cushion or a floor chair or similar product.

I usually have a few low tables I keep my computer on to play music from, as well as to create an altar space on which I place a candle and anything else I wish to contemplate in the journey. I have a large speaker system connected to my computer through a soundboard, but this is probably too big for most people. A high-quality speaker system for a computer is generally more than enough. I prefer speakers over earbuds or headphones because it is exceptionally helpful to feel the extra bass in the room. I like that it's an immersive experience. There are some quality five-or-more-speaker surround-sound systems for computers that can be spread out around the journey mat. Use what you have. It will be good enough.

To prepare for these experiences, you'll want to take a bath or shower, brush your teeth, and put on comfortable clothes. You can meditate, practice yoga, or do other simple stretching exercises. It's also helpful to listen to meditative music while preparing the space. Have fun with the experience.

Here are a few lists of other items you may want to include in your sacred space:

Common Ceremonial Gear

- Ceremonial blanket and/or shawl
- Symbolic items, sacred items, stones, and so on
- Tarot cards, pendulums, and/or other divination tools
- Lavender and other essential oils
- Socks and extra layers of clothing
- Incense, sage, sweetgrass, palo santo, and/or other resins
- Candles
- Rattles and drums

Useful Items for Your Kit

- Small trash can with liner in case you need to vomit
- Tissue and towels
- Lighters and an ashtray for the ash and incenses
- Flashlight, and other illumination tools
- Pipe or vaporizer
- Small first aid kit
- Rescue Remedy and medications (headache medicine and allergy medicine)
- Pure CBD vaporizer and/or nano-encapsulated CBD as a THC antidote

Snacks

- Orange juice
- Chocolate
- Fruit (grapes, strawberries, or raspberries)
- Gluten-free pretzels (crunchy foods are grounding)
- Herbal teas and electrolyte drinks
- Water
- Tip: keep labels near products in group settings in case anyone has allergies

Devoting meaningful attention to your space and your gear is a reflection of your commitment to making your psychedelic cannabis experience intentional and impactful in your life. In the alchemical tradition, everything is a reflection of everything else, so your external "setting" is an important factor that you actually have a lot of agency over. Bringing intentionality to your external world reflects positively into your inner journey experience, increasing you inner agency and providing additional depth of meaning as well. This doesn't mean your space needs to be perfect. Do the best you can and work within your means. It is better to engage in these practices today rather than waiting for a future time where you could have a better space. The most important criterion is your own safety. Once safety is established, allow yourself the acceptance to grow into these practices and allow your space to reflect this evolution and growth as well.

18

Making Music Sets for Psychedelic Cannabis Experiences

Music is one of the most important and meaningful dimensions of these experiences, and it's also one of the more advanced skill sets to develop. It takes time to make great music sets. For that reason, I'm going to share some general recommendations to get you started.

Any online streaming service is fine, but make sure you purchase the premium service to avoid commercials cutting into your practice. I use a simple DJ program a friend of mine recommended, which can be downloaded for free. Music can also be found, purchased, and imported, and most DJ software can pull music directly from streaming services. As our technology evolves, so will our capacity to curate psychedelic experiences.

To get started, figuring out how to use the fade function between songs is extremely important. A good fade is between fifteen and twenty seconds.

I have also developed a few guided meditations that can be downloaded for free from my website, Medicinal Mindfulness (click the Media tab). One of them, the body scan, is a foundational practice that will be discussed in chapter 22. More information can also be found at the back of this book in the "Additional Medicinal Mindfulness Online Resources" section.

MUSIC EQUIPMENT SETUP

I plug my computer into a speaker system with left and right channels and a subwoofer connected through a mixer. A simple and affordable solution is a high-quality computer speaker system. Place the sub at the top of the head and the two small speakers to the right and left of the head, several feet away. This creates an immersive soundscape effect. There are other, more advanced sound systems we use with as many as six speakers and a sub, and these are great for small groups.

Listed below are templates for creating several journeys of differing types and durations.

Template for a One-Set Psychedelic Cannabis Journey (1.5 to 2 hours)

- Background music during preparation
- Smoking ceremony: 10 minutes
- Guided meditation (body scan): 10 to 15 minutes
- Music set: 60 minutes
- Returning meditation: 10 to 15 minutes
- Background music during snacks and reflection/conversations

Template for a Breathwork Journey (1.5 hours)

- Background music during preparation
- Guided meditation (body scan): 10 to 15 minutes (optional)
- First music set: 45 minutes (intense and rhythmic for breathwork facilitation)
- Second music set: 30 to 45 minutes (gentle music for deep relaxation)
- Returning meditation: 10 to 15 minutes
- Background music during snacks and reflection/conversations

Template for a Two-Set Psychedelic Cannabis Journey (2.5 to 3 hours)

- Background music during preparation
- Smoking ceremony: 10 minutes
- Guided meditation (body scan): 10 to 15 minutes
- First music set: 60 minutes
- Bathroom and imbibing break: 10 to 20 minutes
- Second music set: 75 minutes
- Returning meditation: 10 to 15 minutes
- Background music during snacks and reflection/conversations

Template for a Psychedelic Cannabis Breathwork Journey (3 to 3.5 hours)

- Background music during preparation
- Smoking ceremony: 10 minutes
- Guided meditation: 10 to 15 minutes (optional)
- First music set: 45 minutes (intense and rhythmic for breathwork facilitation)
- Second music set: 45 to 60 minutes (gentle music for deep relaxation)
- Optional bathroom and imbibing break: 10 to 20 minutes
- Third music set (optional): 60 to 75 minutes
- Returning meditation: 10 to 15 minutes
- Background music during snacks and reflection/conversations

Example Music Set for a Psychedelic Cannabis Session*

Flute music or other gentle songs for background music during setup or conversations. Fade when ready for smoking ceremony.

Eternal Om by Dick Sutphen—Gentle meditation oms for back-

---

*I believe all or most of this is available through streaming services. More music set samples are provided on our Medicinal Mindfulness website under the Media tab.

ground music during smoking ceremony. Fade when you're ready to lie down.

Crystal Bowls Chakra Chants by Jonathan Goldman or the body scan guided meditation—These provide great background music for guided meditation. Two songs take up about 20 minutes. You'll already be lying down, so you won't want more than 20 minutes of music here.

Weightless by Marconi Union—Transitioning, relaxing, entrancing

Jaguar Dreaming by Liquid Bloom—Rhythmic, deepening, energetic

Legions (Wars) by Zoe Keating—Evocative, strong

Planetarium by Nick Cave and Warren Ellis—Light, uplifting

Ka Ewa Eke by Kimba Arem—Deepening, entrancing

Jewel in the Lotus by Maneesh De Moor—Playful, energetic, deepening

A World Behind the World by Jami Sieber—Uplifting, concluding

Shamanic Dream by Anuguma—Returning meditation for about 20 minutes. Let it fade out as you gently return from the experience.

Flute music—Additional background music to complete the session

GENERAL MUSIC RECOMMENDATIONS

Instead of gentle music rising to an extended peak, then returning to gentle music again at the end, psychedelic cannabis experiences benefit the most from a back and forth between gentle and evocative songs. Most of my songs are about eight minutes long but I also use shorter songs and even series of songs from the same musician to create different themes in the musical flow. My longest songs are about fifteen minutes long. In a solo session, you'll want to create your set beforehand based on the format of the session, set the fades, hit play, and get comfortable. Peer-sitters can mix the sets as they go. This is something I do in my own session work. Psychedelic cannabis is intense enough. Gentle, simple music elicits profound healing states. Evocative music elicits epic journey experiences.

Here are some other suggestions to keep in mind:

- Loud or really intense music isn't always the best option.
- Avoid languages you can understand, unless a song is played for a specific purpose.
- Mix the genres. Not everyone likes every genre of music, but most are okay with a song or two of specific genres.
- Don't go all classical! That's an outdated orientation for psychedelic music facilitation.
- Transition from intense to gentle songs in stages, like ocean waves, instead of one long peak and return.

GETTING STARTED

It is easy to overthink the music. It's okay to play and experiment. Use the sample set to make radio stations based on the AI algorithms of these streaming programs. Listen to and save the music you like from these and make "best of" playlists to experiment with. Combine new music with music you know you love so you're not constantly critiquing the music. Music is like a big projector screen, and it shows you what you need to see. It's a wonderful way to share an experience.

19

Imbibing Cannabis with Intention

The word *imbibe* means "to drink or to fully assimilate into your being." For me, this is how I speak of smoking, vaping, or otherwise consuming cannabis with a sacred or healing intention. I have yet to find a way to say "take a toke" with any sort of depth or meaning. Another way we describe it in ceremony is "we take this breath," and at that moment we light our pipes and smoke. As I've said previously, I've just begun to dive into more potent and longer experiences with edibles and tinctures. And at this time, fundamentally, I don't think using anything but the flower is necessary for deeply healing psychedelic experiences. That said, there are medical and social reasons why smoking or vaping might not be recommended, so tincture- and edible-specific applications and techniques are being developed.

From my point of view, taking the medicine with intention is a centrally important part of the psychedelic cannabis experience. It connects us with the ancient spiritual lineages these medicines are connected to and allows us to speak directly to our inner consciousness, unconscious, and symbolic self in a way that it can understand with grace and ease. Ritual, ceremony, and symbol point to universal, archetypal languages that somehow connect us all.

A simple way to take cannabis with intention is to say a prayer or state an intention before imbibing. A simple example that I use in my own practice is the following:

> *In this good way we invite this sacred plant ally,*
> *Cannabis sativa, into our hearts, our minds, our*
> *bodies, and our spirit for healing and transformation.*
> *Thank you for being available for this journey*
> *experience. In this good way we give thanks.*

Saying this simple statement before imbibing can dramatically change the effects cannabis has on us. It turns it from recreational and sometimes avoidant to deeply meaningful and insightful.

As I developed these practices, I primarily relied on my transpersonal and clinical counseling training, my understanding of Western alchemy and Western mysticism, and my understanding of the teachings regarding the seven sacred directions common in many indigenous traditions—the four cardinal directions, the earth, the sky, and the within. One of the reasons I work solely with cannabis in my practice, besides legality, is to respect the boundaries of my personal ancestry and to avoid the unethical appropriation of someone else's culture. These are complicated issues. I've personally settled on language and skill sets oriented in psychology. However, I've also settled on frameworks from spiritual practices that encourage us to turn toward a feeling of safety within our environment by acknowledging the cardinal directions. This is an almost universal practice in ancient spiritual traditions. The creation of some sort of healing space, which is separate from ordinary space and is perhaps something we dare to call "sacred space," seems pretty essential to reach the highest peaks and deepest meaning in this work.

I developed the Mindful Journeywork practice, an intentional ceremony of imbibing cannabis, to facilitate the importance of ceremony without dogma. It is specifically tied to teachable skill sets within a context that emphasizes visualizing a safe space. It is only provided here as a framework for imbibing if you don't want to employ or establish your own. I have also included discussions and other ceremonies written by other members of our community that have come out of this exploration for you to review and draw from. But again, please feel encouraged to make them your own.

SETTING SACRED SPACE

Setting sacred space combines the aspects of set, setting, and skill into one practice. It's a way to create safety, cultivate awareness, and bring skill and intention to any medicine experience.

The ceremony itself is very archetypal, and some form of this practice exists in most religious and mystical traditions. While it's possible to speak in spiritual and energetic terms, it's also relevant to speak to the power of the imagination to induce different states of mind. In a sense, using the imagination, imagery, symbolism, and words helps program an inner mind state well-resourced for the experience at hand. Setting sacred space is a skill set that can be developed over time to increase personal resilience.

Generally, a circle around the meditation space is drawn with our mind's eye, our imagination, and energetic proprioceptive awareness. Usually, this is done in a clockwise motion starting in the east and proceeding to the south, west, and north and ending back in the east. I call this last section "closing the hatch." Our awareness is then brought to the center, the vertical axis found in the middle of the circle and in the center of our embodied sense of self. Awareness is then turned to either the above, below, and within, or the below, above, and within. The four primary directions represent aspects of self, whereas the vertical axis represents systems larger than the self.

From an energetic paradigm, orienting to the four directions allows us to orient along natural electromagnetic fields, which can create a strong grounding experience. The number 4 is very stable. In a sense, setting sacred space is aligning our own energetic field with the larger collective energetic field of the space, the group (if you're working with one), and the vastly larger field of the Earth, creating a subtle group cohesion that supports intentional experiences.

The number 7 is relevant in many traditions, too, including the seven stages of alchemy, and working with the seven directions also makes sense from a somatic resourcing perspective, regardless of any sort of spiritual significance. Registering safety in all directions, making an intentional observation that your space is safe, helps bring a deeper sense of safety and relaxation to your psychedelic experience.

It is controversial to acknowledge the use of a prayer within a community that has experienced so much trauma in religious contexts. However, prayer combined with the religious or spiritual use of psychedelics is an ancient practice. According to Terence McKenna, the use of psychedelics is possibly older than humanity itself. In a sense, prayer is a reclaiming of an ancient part of ourselves and is sometimes an important part of our healing process.

While this practice comes from religious and mystical traditions, it can also be thought of in terms of developing psychological resiliencies. The directions can be known as the winds, the guardians, the spirits, the energies, the symbols, and so on. It is okay to make this practice your own and work with a cultural orientation congruent with your identity, staying mindful of issues related to cultural appropriation. The sample practices below attempt to demonstrate an internal congruency with alchemy, mindfulness practices, and depth- and ecopsychology. Because my early background consisted of learning from Native American teachers, these traditions are also acknowledged in the structure of these practices. It is the way I was taught to open my practice, but it's not the only way. Some form of "calling in the directions" is a common practice in many underground psychedelic communities. A few great resources for this practice include the books, *Wild Mind* by Bill Plotkin and *Allies for Awakening* by Ralph Metzner.

Speaking out loud to the directions is very powerful. Speaking helps us find our own voice and express our identity, and in group settings, it can induce a very powerful, grounded yet elevated, collective state of mind.

In psychedelic traditions, many practices also invite the "spirit of the medicine" being consumed. Doing so while setting sacred space is a very intentional way to take a medicine, and it can relax the body and mind before doing so, increasing the likelihood of a more positive experience. I also always call in the "transformational power of my breath" to remind me to breathe.

The symbolism of each direction can be very culturally specific. There's no right or wrong way here necessarily, but it's important to remain mindful of issues of cultural appropriation. This is also a very personal process and very private. Who can judge what symbols our soul is drawn to? It's alright to bring elements from many different traditions and systems, including scientific and psychological paradigms. Make the practice relevant and meaningful to you. Above all else, speak from your heart and cultivate a deep gratitude for having the opportunity to create sacred space.

Closing a sacred space is as important as opening it. Acknowledging the directions with gratitude as a closing ceremony after the journey helps bring closure to the experience and begin the integration process. It's generally much shorter than the opening ceremony, but it allows us to bookend the experience so we can rest more deeply.

When I began to develop a practice around cannabis, there were practical things to consider, like when to imbibe, but this practice has evolved to be my own expression of speaking to Spirit.

At this point, I personally don't engage in medicine work anymore without speaking to these intentions in some way. Sometimes, when I'm working with a new client without a lot of experience, I often suggest they imbibe a few times to step gently into the journey space. Sometimes, the journey takes off a little more quickly than expected before the space can be set intentionally. It's always a rocky ride, and I've learned to pause the experience and briefly call in the directions in some manner before going further with the process. After doing so, the experience begins to stabilize immediately.

There's something about orienting to the cardinal directions that feels exceptionally ancient and universally human. All cultures do it. The Mindful Journeywork practice below is a way to imbibe with intention that orients to this ancient practice in a way that feels as culturally neutral as possible. Get out your phone or a compass and learn where the directions are in your space. It's time to start connecting to our environment again.

When you and your space are ready, turn on some gentle music, load your pipe, and begin. Start centering yourself by connecting with your breath and feeling your body. Choose to breathe into your belly a little more deeply than you were before. The first time you state, "I still myself and breathe," close your eyes, and take a deep breath. Then, in each of the next sections when you repeat the words, "I still myself and breathe," it's an invitation to either take another deep breath or take some of the medicine. Smaller tokes are better than big ones because they're less hard on the throat and lungs, and you're invited to take as many tokes as you need to. I recommend having cough drops or tea for sore throats handy as well. These can really help. Remember, we're in the realm of subjective dosing. Take what you need to. If you want, start light or pause the prayer and go as slowly as you want to. Maybe for the first few times you imbibe with intention, focus primarily on dosage in this step. This could take as little as thirty seconds to a minute between each statement, or as long as five minutes or more if this is the primary intention of the first journey. Using the practice below, going slowly and enjoying the directions while smoking, is a wonderful way to start. If you are leading a group, simply adjust the pronouns used to address the participants.

Meditation for the
Mindful Journeywork Practice

You are encouraged to speak these statements out loud as you meditate on the meaning, pause after each line "I still myself and breathe" and either take a breath, imbibe the medicine, or both. Slow the process down and enjoy the experience.

I still myself and breathe.

Turning my awareness to the east,
I bring focused awareness to my present-moment experience.
I still myself and breathe.

Turning my awareness to the south,
I remain curious about sensations in my body and energetic field.
I still myself and breathe.

Turning my awareness to the west,
I feel fully and allow the inner journey to unfold all around me.
I still myself and breathe.

Turning my awareness to the north,
I discern my thoughts and harvest insight, understanding, and
mastery.
I still myself and breathe.

Turning my awareness to the below,
I center in the support of my ancestors and of this sacred Earth.
I still myself and breathe.

Turning my awareness to the above,
I rise up to explore infinite possibility.
I still myself and breathe.

Turning my awareness within,
I manifest my calling in this life for the benefit of all beings.
I still myself and breathe.

I am my own teacher.
I am my own guide.
I take full responsibility for this experience.
I am grateful for this opportunity to be present in sacred space.

In this good way, I give thanks.

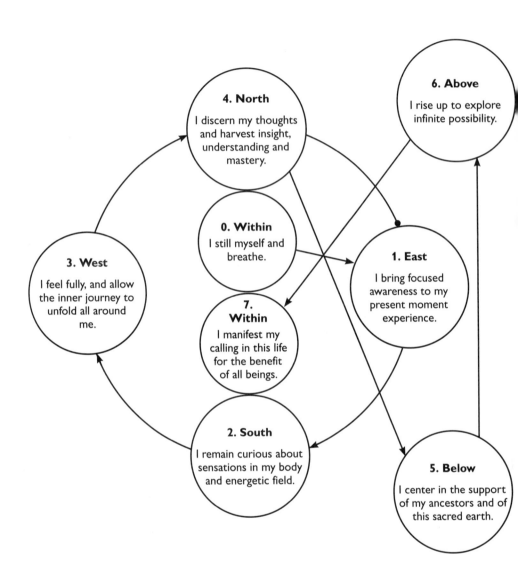

4. North

I discern my thoughts and harvest insight, understanding and mastery.

6. Above

I rise up to explore infinite possibility.

0. Within

I still myself and breathe.

3. West

I feel fully, and allow the inner journey to unfold all around me.

1. East

I bring focused awareness to my present moment experience.

7. Within

I manifest my calling in this life for the benefit of all beings.

2. South

I remain curious about sensations in my body and energetic field.

5. Below

I center in the support of my ancestors and of this sacred earth.

You can see from this diagram that the symbolism
of the seven directions and the four primary medicine practices
are embedded in the ceremony.

GRATITUDE PRAYER

The following prayer is what I use when I personally take the medicine and when I lead groups. I have found the longer prayer provides about enough time to calm any irritations in the throat between smoking moments. It was the first way I learned how to pray when I was younger, besides trips to church, and there are clear Native American influences here. I have tried my best to be respectful of these traditions. Like many of us, I'm an orphan when it comes to having my own spiritual lineage. This particular prayer is a very intimate expression of my own personal healing practice. I won't go into it here, but there's also an embedded symbolism of transformational alchemy present. Please adjust as needed to make it your own. If you are leading a group, simply adjust the pronouns used to address the participants.

Gratitude Prayer

Begin this sacred ceremony by bringing your awareness to your breath, taking a moment to feel your body and your connection with the Earth. Then, in each of the next sections when you repeat the words "In this good way, I take this breath, I take this medicine, in honor of the spirit of the [direction]," it's an invitation to either take a deep breath or take some of the medicine. Now say the following out loud or to yourself:

At this time, I call in this sacred plant ally, Cannabis sativa, into my heart, my mind, my body, and my spirit for healing and transformation. Thank you for making yourself available in this way. I also invite the transformational power of my breath. Thank you for this opportunity to share sacred space.

East

Now bring your awareness to the east and say the following:

I call upon the spirit of the east. Spirit of new beginnings and clear vision. Thank you so much for this capacity to see clearly and to remain focused in this experience. I am so grateful for your presence in this circle. In this good way, I take this breath, I take this medicine, in honor of the spirit of the east.

South

Draw your awareness to the south and say the following:

I call upon the spirit of the south. Spirit of curiosity, joy, and play. Thank you for reminding me to play, even in the deep spaces of the work. I'm so grateful for your presence in this circle. In this good way I take this breath, I take this medicine, in honor of the spirit of the south.

West

Draw your awareness to the west and say the following:

I call upon the spirit of the west. Spirit of introspection and intuition, the dreamtime and the imagination, passing through the deep places of the soul. Thank you for being with me in this sacred place. I am so grateful for your presence in this circle. In this good way, I take this breath, I take this medicine, in honor of the spirit of the west.

North

Draw your awareness to the north and say the following:

I call upon the spirit of the north. Spirit of wisdom, of knowing through experience, and of the inner warrior, teacher, elder, and healer. Thank you for teaching me and guiding me on this journey. I am so grateful for your presence in this circle. In this good way, I take this breath, I take this medicine, in honor of the spirit of the north.

East to Center

Draw your awareness back to the east and say the following:

Closing the hatch, completing the circle, I step into the center. The vertical axis. The center of both this space and the center of myself.

Below

Draw your energy down through your being and into the center of the Earth and say the following:

I call upon the spirit below. Spirit of abundance. Spirit of my ancestors and the ancestors of this sacred land. Be with me now in this sacred space. Thank you for supporting me and centering me in this sacred space. I am so grateful. In this good way, I take this breath, I take this medicine, in honor of the spirit below.

Above

Draw your awareness up now from the center of the Earth and through your being and direct it upward toward the sky, the center of the universe, and say the following:

I call upon the spirit above. Spirit of inspiration. Spirit of the cosmos and all that is, unity consciousness, the One Mind, and future possibilities. Thank you so much for inspiring me to take this journey. In this good way, I take this breath, I take this medicine, in honor of the spirit above.

Within

Draw your awareness down now and into your body and say the following:

I step into that center-most place of myself. The core of my being. In this good way, I call upon the spirit within. The deepest and highest aspects of myself. That which led me to this very moment. The witness. Thank you so much for being with me in this sacred space. I am so grateful. In this good way, I take this breath, I take this medicine, in honor of the spirit within.

Honoring Allies

I take this time to call upon all of my allies, guides, and ancestors, known and unknown, here to support me in this space. Thank you for being with me and supporting me. I am so grateful. In this good way, I take this breath in honor of my allies. (At this time, you are invited to smoke as much as you wish, trusting your body and intuition.) In this good way, I give thanks.

Closing the Ceremony

At the completion of the ceremony, it's important to acknowledge the seven directions again and any themes from the ceremony that came up in relationship to aspects of that direction. This reinforces to the psyche that the session is over. Say the following:

In this good way, I take this moment to give thanks to the sacred directions for being with me and for supporting me on this journey. Thank you so much spirit of the east, spirit of _____ [insert a descriptor mentioned in the beginning for the east, such as "new beginnings" or "clear vision."] I am grateful for your presence in this circle. Thank you spirit of the south, spirit of _____. I am so grateful. Thank you spirit of the west, spirit of _____. Thank you spirit of the north, spirit of _____. Thank you spirit below, spirit of _____. Spirit above, spirit of _____. Spirit within, spirit of _____. I am so grateful for your presence in this circle. At this time, I give thanks to all of my ancestors and guides, allies and healers who were with me on this journey. I give thanks to [list energies, archetypes, symbols, totems, etc. that were mentioned in the beginning or manifested strongly in the experience]. Thank you transformational power of my own breath. Thank you plant ally, Cannabis sativa. I am so grateful. In this good way, I give thanks.

SEVEN CHAKRAS MEDITATION

The seven chakras meditation is a wonderful alternative to the seven directions meditation in the gratitude prayer and is popular with yoga practitioners. I usually start at the crown chakra and work my way down to the root, with every chakra offering an opportunity to take more medicine. I like to think of this as the more grounded you become in the body, the higher you get with the medicine. A student of mine who practices ganja yoga starts at the root and goes to the crown.

Seven Chakras Meditation

Begin by bringing your awareness to your crown, the top of the head, and continue down through the other six chakras as you say the following:

Bringing my awareness to my crown, a beautiful violet color, I give thanks for my capacity to connect with the Divine. In this good way, I take this medicine honoring my connection to the Divine.

Bringing my awareness to my third eye, a beautiful indigo color, I give thanks for my capacity to see clearly. In this good way, I take this medicine honoring my spiritual vision.

Bringing my awareness to my throat, a beautiful sky blue, I give thanks for my capacity to speak my truth and to be fully self-expressed. In this good way, I take this medicine honoring my self-expression.

Bringing my awareness to my heart, center of compassion, a beautiful emerald green, I give thanks for my capacity to accept myself and to feel love. In this good way, I take this medicine honoring my heart.

Bringing my awareness to my solar plexus, a beautiful sun yellow, I give thanks for my capacity of will and my ability to accomplish. In this good way, I take this medicine honoring my solar plexus.

Bringing my awareness to my lower belly, a beautiful fiery orange, I give thanks for my creativity and my sexuality. In this good way, I give thanks for my capacity to create.

Bringing my awareness to my hips and sacrum, my root, a beautiful ruby red, I give thanks for my physical body and the world I live in. In this good way, I give thanks for my foundation.

PART FOUR

The Captain Protocol

A Family of Practices for
Using Psychedelic Cannabis
for Healing

◆◆◆

The Captain Protocol was developed from years of exploring the realm of guided psychedelic cannabis sessions. In a solo practice, it comprises a family of exercises that help journeyers develop their sense of agency— not only in psychedelic spaces but also in their lives.

We define the term *agency* as "the ability to respond with skill and discernment to any situation." The loss of agency in unsafe situations often contributes to the accumulation of trauma in the body. A loss of agency in psychedelic medicine experiences is quite common, but this letting go is done in a safe environment in clinical and spiritual settings. Cannabis is a little different from other psychedelics in that at the doses we're working with in this book, it's more common that we keep our agency. In some ways, because cannabis requires us to engage in certain mindfulness practices to elicit full psychedelic experiences, we can generally stop and pause the experience as needed. This is why it's a perfect tool for trauma resolution. Trauma, at its core, is the lack of choice in a difficult situation; therefore, healing trauma involves having choice over what happens next, when it happens, and at what pace.

The purpose of this book is to introduce cannabis as a psychedelic and to demonstrate how to use it for healing, especially for those who might not have access to traditional psychedelics or psychedelic therapy. Therefore chapter 20, "Important Concepts," explores psychology terms typically encountered in psychedelic states. If you are imbibing psychedelic cannabis without a guide or therapist, I am hopeful you'll find the inclusion of this chapter helpful. The chapters that follow provide exercises to discover and build your inner capacities. By doing so, you'll reach automaticity for skillfully exploring psychedelic states. These exercises constitute the foundational practices of the Captain Protocol.

When I started exploring cannabis as a psychedelic intentionally, I was hoping for a legal training tool that *sort of* exhibited psychedelic qualities. We quickly learned that when cannabis is used the right way, it can offer just as intense a psychedelic experience as other psychedelic medicines. Because of this, it appears to be just as useful, and maybe even more so for some people, as other psychedelic medicines—psilocybin, LSD, DMT, ayahuasca, and the empathogen MDMA—for psychedelic healing purposes.

In a therapeutic setting, MDMA, for example, automatically elicits certain natural processes in the body and mind for healing purposes. These automatic processes mimic mindfulness practices that can be taught, practiced, developed, and used to heal the same symptoms when used in conjunction with psychedelic cannabis. Working with psychedelic cannabis is *almost* automatic. These practices are very easy to incorporate, and powerful, evocative cannabis experiences should be pretty immediate. In fact, I'd like to invite you to slow the practice way down to step into the practice gradually, to increase your confidence in navigating inner spaces and to reduce the risks associated with jumping right in.

In a sense, you're developing your own inner capacity for self-healing and implementing this into a practice that facilitates and amplifies that natural process. Cannabis appears to make this skill development possible.

20

Important Concepts

Before we start exploring the important concepts of the Captain Protocol, it would be useful to have a shared vocabulary. Having language that explicitly describes and correctly frames the nature of psychedelic cannabis experiences allows us to further discern the gifts of these practices and to better develop them. These concepts are also important in understanding the sometimes invisible nature of the experiences so that we feel safe enough to enter them as deeply as is often required to complete a transformational process.

MINDFULNESS AND MINDFUL JOURNEYWORK

Our program uses the term *Mindful Journeywork,* bringing mindfulness practices into psychedelic journey experiences to explore a particular intention (this is the "work" part of the journeywork). But what is mindfulness? Christopher Germer, in the introduction to *Mindfulness and Psychotherapy,* defines mindfulness simply as an "awareness of present experience with acceptance." Breaking this simple definition down brings us certain characteristics we want to highlight. *Awareness* implies bringing your focus to a phenomenon and bringing your conscious attention to it. *Present experience* refers to it happening right now, as opposed to being in the past or the future. Everything happens in the present moment. For example, a memory of the past is experienced as something in the present by bringing attention to your body's response to the memory and your present emotions. *Acceptance* means yielding to the nature of your awareness as perceptive of only the present moment. You might land in some difficult territory, such as a big emotion or a difficult memory. Acceptance allows us to remain curious about what we're experiencing. Resisting an experience causes friction and takes energy. When we accept that we're having an experience and allow it to happen, this allows the holotropic nature of the healing process to unfold. Resisting, or turning away from, a particular experience stops this process from unfolding. Skillfully pausing the process is called titration and is more of a slowing down, or a kind of distant observation, than an avoidance or turning away from.

Journeywork is the active participation within the dreamlike realm of our inner state, our memories, feelings, and sensations, as well as transpersonal spaces that appear to be populated by things that transcend the self and four-dimensional space-time. While it can be accurately described as an inner experience, it often feels like we're immersed in a process bigger than ourselves.

Journeywork is defined by the dictionary as "necessary, routine, and menial work." It is something done over and over again to produce an outcome bigger than its component parts, a skillful application of simple tasks that when repeated with intention can create something significant. I like to think of something like building a piece of furniture. Cutting wood, sanding it, drilling holes, and gluing pegs are all journeywork skills but combined with the intention of creating a chair. You can't skip the work of building a chair if you want to eventually end up with a chair. The same is true with psychedelics. However, in a psychedelic state, you can experience an image of the chair you want to make, and feel what it's like to have it, before you begin the labor.

Mindful Journeywork is the system of repetitive mindfulness tasks that lead to healing, awakening, and agency in psychedelic states. Lucky for us, in psychedelic states, these repetitive tasks can be incredibly interesting to engage in. If you're bored, this is a clear indication that you are ready to step deeper into the practice.

THREE AREAS OF DEVELOPMENT

An ongoing practice of meditation helps us develop certain inner capacities, which I discuss in detail in the next chapter. These capacities can be summarized in three interrelated categories: skill, resilience, and power.

Skill is the required knowledge and particular ability to respond to an experience or to manifest something you want to create. For example, painting a portrait requires skill sets around using brushes, paint, and other artist's tools, as well as knowledge of proportions and anatomy. Someone skillful in a particular art form is called an artist. The same goes for being a medical doctor. A doctor's skill set includes the knowledge required to be a healer but also all of the practical skills of being a doctor. When we apply skill to mindfulness practices and psychedelic spaces, we gain the capacity to heal trauma, turn toward difficult material, and wake up to ourselves. Having more skill in our lives gives us a greater sense of agency.

Resilience is the ability to tolerate, accept, and recover from an experience that requires effort to explore. Resilience is the capacity, for example, to stay with a difficult emotion or memory to complete the process of transforming that memory. If we don't have resilience, we have to go at a slower pace. It is like walking a mile, for example, if we don't have the endurance to run it. We still get to the same place, but slower. Resilience and endurance are closely related. Some people have stronger capacities to handle difficult inner content or to recover from something that required great effort. Resilience also points to toughness. In martial arts practices, for example, it's the capacity to be challenged by an opponent and to take the blows without being seriously hurt. Having more resilience in our lives gives us a greater sense of agency.

Power is the ability to transmute, transform, or create a particular experience within a given time frame. For example, someone who can climb a mountain in a day is more powerful than someone who can climb the same mountain in a week. Power is the capacity to transform your experience of the present moment into something you desire. Whereas resilience may be a passive state, a quality of being, power is an active state, a quality of doing. The faster you can move through something, the more powerful you are. Engaging in processes that help you clear what you want to clear and develop what you want to develop is closely related to personal empowerment. Power isn't about having control over another. That's more closely related to force and coercion. Having more power in our lives gives us a greater sense of agency.

Skillful practice allows us to turn a skillful action into an automatic response. A pianist doesn't have to think about playing a piano skillfully. Through practice, a skillful pianist can play incredibly complex and beautiful arrangements automatically, being fully present in the moment, while enjoying the experience. The same can be said about any mindfulness practice or Mindful Journeywork practice. This skill set is called *psychedelic agency*. When cannabis is used skillfully as a psychedelic, this skill set of agency can translate to other psychedelic medicines.

The following list provides examples of useful capacities for healing in psychedelic spaces:

- Extreme emotional tolerance
- Ability to handle stress
- Ability to focus in disorienting states
- Ability to perceive, navigate, and remember/report back
- Mental stability with openness
- Physical and psychological stamina and resilience
- Ability to clear trauma/dross
- Ability to confront the "shadow," or difficult aspects of self
- Compassionate communication in shared experience

TRANSMUTATION AND THE
HOLOTROPIC NATURE OF REALITY
AND THE SELF

It is important to let go of trying to fix yourself or get rid of the aspects of your humanness you consider *bad*. Instead, it's important to think of movement toward health and the *transmutation* of an experience into its highest expression. For example, there's very little difference between anxiety and excitement—the first has a negative connotation associated with it, and the second a positive one. What if we could reorient more positively to all aspects of who we are and our emotional states by framing them in a different way?

Dr. Stanislav Grof, one of the early LSD researchers and founder of transpersonal psychology, coined the term *holotropic,* meaning the natural movement toward wholeness and healing. Holotropic is a term similar to *heliotropic,* which is a plant's natural movement and growth toward sunlight. The holotropic nature of reality and the self implies that if we could only get out of the way of a healing process, in a contained and safe setting, then healing, health, awakening, and the transmutation to these states happens on its own. From this perspective, all we're doing here is supporting or further facilitating the process with skillful action.

THE WITNESS AND
THE INNER HEALING INTELLIGENCE

There is an innate, intrinsic, inner aspect we all have that is directly in contact with this holotropic nature of the universe. Sometimes it gets covered up, and we don't have access to it, but if we listen and allow, this aspect will begin to speak to us through intuition, curiosity, and a sense of wonder and amazement. In many spiritual traditions, this aspect is called the *witness*. It's this part of ourselves that can watch what's happening objectively and without attachment, while simultaneously providing insights and new understandings in how to turn the situation toward a holotropic process. Grof calls this capacity the *inner healing intelligence,* or the *inner radar.* This inner healing intelligence or radar knows exactly what we're ready to turn toward and heal as the next step in our transformational process. Even if it's difficult, a process just wouldn't show up if we weren't ready to work with it.

INTUITION

The innate healing intelligence speaks to us through something called our intuition. Our intuition is the developed capacity to know the truth of something without knowing why we know it. The answers come from some place deep inside ourselves and not via a rational linear process we have to work out step-by-step. We just know. Again, intuition isn't something you either have or don't have; it's a skill set that can be developed.

THE CENTRAL IMPORTANCE OF THE IMAGINATION

The imagination is one of the most underutilized resources we have as human beings. Our capacity to imagine something is the ability to explore complex information through a simplified visual representation. Imagination is different from fantasy and escapism. It is an internal resource. If your unconscious mind wants to tell you something important, it will do so through symbols rather than words. Symbolism is an ancient and archetypal language. The symbolic meaning of the images seen in these inner experiences provides important information for our transformational experience and healing. It is like the subconscious is trying to directly communicate exactly what we need to know but the translator mechanism is sometimes glitched by our own misinterpretations. When we begin to clear trauma and develop these capacities, we begin to understand this language more clearly. (In alchemy, this is called the *true imagination.*)

Visualization and imagination also support us in facilitating transformational processes for healing. If you can imagine or see something in your mind's eye, you can imagine engaging in different processes. These processes offer real results in our healing.

PARTS AND ASPECTS OF SELF

Human beings are complex, and our inner world reflects this complexity. Our inner voice isn't necessarily singular; we have internalized messages and assumptions that come from places so complex they almost feel like completely different personalities. This is often referred to as the *multiplicity of the psyche*. Sometimes our inner voice even sounds different at times—younger, older, feminine, masculine, judgmental, or accepting. It's very complex in there. Learning to differentiate between aspects of self, to get to know them and accept them, is part of the healing and waking up process. Some aspects are quite wonderful, and some are quite wounded. Sometimes these wounded parts of ourselves can lash out and sabotage something that has great meaning and importance in our lives. We are each required to turn toward these parts, called *shadow* aspects, and to shine the light of self-acceptance and compassion on them, to return them to our inner family of acceptance.

To explore the alchemy of aspects of self in-depth, I recommend the books *Greater Than the Sum of Our Parts* by Richard Schwartz and *Wild Mind* by Bill Plotkin.

SHADOW AND SHADOW WORK

Shadow is defined as "an aspect of self that has been disowned or unacknowledged." This doesn't necessarily mean it is a negative trait, just one that is perceived as negative. Someone could just as easily have a gentle, loving tendency that is avoided or unacknowledged as a violent one. Both are shadow. Because a shadow part is unacknowledged, it is usually maladaptive, or injured, so it acts out in ways that sabotage us to get our attention. It is asking to be healed. We can't fully suppress shadow. It has to be expressed in one way or another. It is an instrumental and vital part of ourselves.

Carl Jung referred to shadow as the "gold in the dark." I like that analogy. I also use the phrase "gems in the dark." Sometimes the healing process requires us to look at difficult material, but within this material are sparkling little gems of soul parts waiting to be reclaimed and reawakened. Shadow work is waking up work. Waking up means waking up to all aspects of ourselves, not just the good or pretty ones. You know you are dealing with shadow material when the journey feels edgy or difficult. This is good news and means you are making significant progress. Take your time, go slow, and be gentle with yourself. Embedded in the darkest spots of our psyches are our greatest gifts, waiting to be uncovered. These processes always complete in an empowered state of being.

To explore aspects of self and shadow with cannabis is an advanced technique, but it can sometimes come up early in the process, particularly in the form of judgmental voices. It is possible to think of these judgments as old scripts and a form of mental dross that can be cleared through compassionate awareness. Because of this, shadow work is an important part of both the healing and waking-up process. To learn more about shadow and how to work with it, I recommend the book *The Dark Side of the Light Chasers* by Debbie Ford.

DROSS AND TRAUMA

Dross is a term used in transformational alchemy and historically was used to describe the crusty stuff removed in the purification process of a substance. The term is used here to describe something in our system that inhibits our capacities as human beings. It is basically *stuckness* in all its multitude of forms. It can literally be experienced as a substance with unique sensory/perceptive properties that once acknowledged can either be cleared out of the body or transmuted and transformed into usable energy.

Clearing dross is a regular and ongoing practice. Eventually, it becomes something akin to flossing your teeth. Symptoms of trauma can be considered an accumulation of dross. Early on in our healing process, any step toward progress may feel overwhelming because we have accumulated a lot of dross and have never learned to discharge it. Working with psychedelic cannabis, MDMA, and other psychedelics helps facilitate the removal of dross from our system.

Symptoms of Dross in Humans

Awareness of a symptom is an experience of an energetic discharge "halfway out" or leaving your system. Any sensation or perception in these holotropic experiences is a symptom of dross leaving your body and your consciousness. This is the holotropic nature of our psyche. Trusting the process and relaxing around it allows the symptom to discharge and release. Holding it, suppressing it, or avoiding the sensation of it, keeps it stuck.

The following are examples of dross symptoms:

- Physical tension, pain, and disease—energetic kinks in the fascia
- Unwanted emotional and psychological patterns—shame, fear, anxiety, anger, or grief
- Unwanted thoughts, delusions, compulsions, judgments, or belief systems
- Toxins and pharmaceutical residues
- Energetic blocks in meridians and chakras
- Symbolic and archetypal manifestations
- Ancestral and past-life karma
- External factors such as oppression, -isms, and barriers to reaching our full potential (personal resources, education, and so on)

Discharges and Contractions

Unusual energetic or physical sensations, such as twitching, burning, buzzing, spasming, vibrating, shaking, tensing up and releasing, hypothermia-like trembling, popping, and so on, denote moments of energetic discharge. A discharge is when a big clump of different symptoms releases at once, and although very weird or intense at times, it's a really good thing. It's the visceral experience of an old, stuck memory and emotional cluster finally getting unstuck and leaving the body. If something like this starts happening, allow your awareness to stay with it and relax into and all around it until it passes. Most importantly, don't intentionally move; stay with the spontaneous movement and let it happen. Sometimes these movements may be accompanied by an intense emotion, a memory, or both (an emotionally charged memory). Or they may be accompanied by symbolic/archetypal imagery.

Sometimes a symptom will intensify before it subsides, so it may feel like the opposite of healing is happening, when in fact, this is what healing looks like. This is called a contraction. It's similar to the birthing process where a muscle will begin to spasm and then intensify before it releases through a discharge. The key to a contraction and discharge is to relax into the experience and allow it to happen while gently witnessing with self-acceptance and compassion.

PSYCHEDELIC SYNESTHESIA

Psychedelic experiences have a tendency to combine sensations and thoughts in unusual ways. These tendencies fall into two categories: synesthesia and ideasthesia. Synesthesia is literally the "union of senses." When one sensory or cognitive pathway leads to an autonomic, involuntary experience in a second sensory or cognitive pathway, we experience synesthesia. A common form of synesthesia is *seeing* music or sound in the form of colorful patterns. Another is pairing emotions with visual components as in the saying, "I'm so *angry,* I'm seeing *red!*" Ideasthesia is a phenomenon in which activations of concepts evoke perception-like experiences. For example, when you think of a particular number, it might always show up in your mind as a particular color.

A primary form of synesthesia in psychedelic therapy work is a somatic sensation coupled with an activated inner process. This awareness of sensations in our bodies is called somatic awareness, and the ability to name and discern what's going on is called somatic intelligence. The capacity to feel into the body, to sense the tension and relaxation there, as well as where a body part is in location to another body part, is called proprioception.

A very useful and interesting form of synesthesia is something I've come to call visual proprioception, which is the combination of an inner visual and imaginal capacity with our physical, felt sense. Visual proprioception is experienced as seeing inside the body and is a common effect of psychedelic cannabis. When this happens, we can have a direct experience of something called the *light body*.

Psychedelic synesthesia is the direct combination of all forms of psychedelic sensing into one cohesive experience, and it can be quite the ride. If you have ever taken a psychedelic, you may know what I'm talking about. Psychedelic synesthesia is a full immersion—body, mind, and soul—into something that feels bigger than the self. It is a primary goal of the psychedelic medicine practice. I discuss this form of synesthesia in the "Five Awareness Practice" in chapter 24.

The Light Body

The light body is a somatic and often visual representation of our physical form with profound psychedelic awareness. Boundaries between the inside and the outside begin to warp as we see that perhaps an entire universe lives within us. With this greater awareness, we can sense/feel/see energy moving through our bodies along meridians, feel energy centers that may correspond to concepts like chakras, and even feel an awareness of an energetic form greater than our physical form, such as our electromagnetic field or aura.

When visual proprioception comes online, we can actually see the light body, as a matrix-like structure of different colored lights and densities (solid, fluid, soft, hard) superimposed on the sensation of the physical body. The light body may also show up in symbolic form to represent aspects of the self, such as images of sacred tools, geometric forms, animal spirits, or other archetypes.

In psychedelic experiences, proprioception isn't limited to our physical bodies, and the perception of proprioception, being part of something we're immersed in, can extend far beyond our understanding of a material form. If psychedelic experiences elicit something that transcends this realm, the light body is what we use to travel through psychedelic states. If it's just symbolic, the image of our own light body still provides a significant amount of necessary information for our own healing and development.

Dross and the Light Body

Unfortunately, we are not all that clear, and dross has generally gummed up our systems. Dross, as an energetic substance, blocks the fluidity and openness of the light body and makes our light bodies heavier and harder to maneuver in our inner experience as well as our outer experience of moving through life. This is a different way of framing the impact trauma has on our bodies and minds. If dross is a substance, it can be cleared and transmuted, possibly used constructively as fuel for transformation or something that can be literally removed and recycled. When visual proprioception comes online, we can *see* dross in our physical bodies as dark, hard, spiky spots in our light body. There is usually some sense of dread or alarm associated with them. Clearing dross from the light body requires sustained effort. That said, significant relief comes with the movement toward wholeness during the process of removing dross, not just after the full process is complete.

Working through dross can feel like an endless, or even hopeless, experience. This is a defense mechanism of the psyche and is simply false. Sometimes this hopelessness intensifies right before a major release, the equivalent of an emotional contraction before it moves through and out of the body. Remember to turn toward the possibility of the holotropic nature of the self and the universe. Remaining curious about your experience allows you to relax into it.

YOU AND THE HOLOTROPIC NATURE OF PSYCHEDELICS AND CANNABIS

Using psychedelics and cannabis for relief, healing, and curiosity is a natural, healthy, human process. Your interest in this work is part of the holotropic nature of a universe you're intimately close to and an important part of. While you may feel some shame or judgment about your interest in cannabis and psychedelics, these feelings are a form of emotional dross, which you can also clear. You don't have to take my word for it, either. You can test this yourself through these practices. You are way more than what you've been told you are by society.

The Five
Inner Capacities

Healing and awakening happen in the body. Every human being has a natural capacity to navigate holotropic states, but like any capacity, it's a skill developed over time and used with greater and greater accuracy and power. I've categorized five primary inner capacities important to psychedelic cannabis experiences. All of them are related to the body.

Five Inner Capacities

1. Somatic awareness and breath
2. Focused awareness and inner visual acuity
3. Allowing, accepting, and relaxing into (trusting) the process
4. Understanding and discernment
5. Curiosity, creativity, and play

Engaging in the foundational practices discussed here and in the next chapter, both separately and in conjunction with psychedelic cannabis and breathwork, helps to develop and fine-tune them. The more you practice, the easier it will be to focus on all of these capacities simultaneously, which will then allow you to deepen your relationship with the Captain Protocol. The goal of this practice is to make the capacities automatic so you can skillfully navigate extreme psychedelic states. Before we go any further, let's define them in more detail and explore them with exercises.

SOMATIC AWARENESS AND BREATH

Breath awareness is a form of somatic awareness. Breath occurs in the body, and knowing how you are breathing, including the depth of your breath and the subtle energetic sensations around your breathing, requires an awareness of body sensations in your face, throat, sternum, back, ribcage, diaphragm, and lungs. Emotional qualities are also present in the felt sense of breath. Breathing with intention creates shifts in sensation within our body that we most want to be aware of. It is the awareness of these shifting somatic sensations, as we breathe, which is the most healing.

Breathing is often synonymous with relaxing, and we experience this relaxation in the body as well. It is difficult to relax around a sensation if we lack awareness of the tension we hold or can't breathe with it. Breathing intentionally is the mechanism that relaxes these tensions. Because our breath is in our bodies, somatic awareness and breath are intimately interrelated.

Somatic Awareness

The sense we use in these practices is a type of somatic awareness called proprioception, as mentioned earlier. Proprioception is derived from the Latin *proprius,* meaning "one's own," and the English word *(re)ception.* Proprioception is a felt sense of a location in the body and the effort being employed there. In other words, we sense tension and relaxation through our proprioceptive sense. Proprioception is our *inner* sense, the awareness of our own bodies. It can also act as an inner spotlight we can use to explore the sensations in specific locations throughout our bodies. It's also the awareness we have of a body part's location in relation to other parts of the body as well as our surroundings.

❦ Proprioception Exercise I

Bring your awareness to your left pinky. Now your right big toe. Now both at the same time. You can sense where these two locations are spatially to each other and the world, as well as how much tension or exertion you're holding in them.

Try doing this with other parts of the body. Try holding different positions and relax the tense areas in the body. What do you notice, and how do you notice it? This is proprioception, or the beginning of somatic awareness.

💗 Proprioception Exercise 2

Find a partner and take turns mirroring each other's movements. Notice your awareness of your own body as you track the experience of your partner's. We can *travel* through our body in the vehicle of our own awareness and shine light (awareness) on and into our body (skin, muscle, bones, organs, brain, and so forth) not only to perceive what's happening there but to actively engage it to relax, surrender, and heal.

Breath

Breath is our greatest ally; it's always with us. Breathing equals acceptance and naturally relaxes the body. It is the engine of transformation.

You may forget to breathe at times, and that's okay; just go back to the deeper breathing when you can. This breath is intentional but not forced. Find the edge of comfort and don't go past it. Breath can also be used to titrate, or slow down, the inner experience (it can also speed it up). If you're in an area that's uncomfortable, you can slow down the breath to reduce the intensity or deepen the breath to move through it more quickly. A common practice is to imagine *breathing into* a part of the body as you bring awareness to it. That means to imagine the energy from the breath traveling not only to your lungs but through them and filling the area of the body you're focusing on.

Most humans breathe shallowly into the chest, even sometimes into only the upper chest, then hold their breath or stop breathing altogether when they're stressed or afraid. Instead of stopping to breathe, learn to breathe more deeply and intentionally into the belly when you're in these situations. Belly breathing is one of the most important aspects of these practices and cannot be overemphasized. Breathing into the belly is a transformational breath that moves an experience forward. Practicing this makes it an automatic response.

❦ Breath Exercise 1

Lie flat on your back with one hand resting on your belly, and the other on your chest. Take deep breaths into your belly. A deep belly breath will raise the belly hand first, then move the hand on the chest. A relaxed belly breath may only raise the hand on the belly. If you're moving the hand on your chest first, or only the chest, this isn't the breath used in these practices. Try different rates of breathing and witness the differences in your body experience.

Some people breathe backward. They push their bellies in when they're taking a breath in and push their bellies out when they're breathing out. If you're doing this, bring extra attention to your breath and learn to breathe the right way. Allow your belly to push outward as you're breathing in and let it relax as you're breathing out. Take time throughout the day to bring attention to your breath.

❦ Breath Exercise 2

Explore *breathing into* an area of the body. Bring your awareness to your feet, then breathe into your feet, imagining that they are being filled with an expansive, relaxing, and revitalizing breath and energy, something like a fresh breeze. Do this a few times in several areas of your body. What do you notice about your experience?

❦ Breath Exercise 3

Try taking a big breath instead of holding your breath when you're startled or scared. If you catch yourself holding your breath, take a few moments and bring some awareness and intention to breathing gently into your belly.

❦ Breath Exercise 4

In any psychedelic experience, turn your awareness to breathing intentionally. Try breathing faster, slower, deeper, or shallower into the belly and into the chest and see how it affects your mental and emotional state.

Getting to know your breath is like developing a new friendship. It takes time but it eventually becomes more nuanced, more powerful, even richer. It's hard to describe, but if you keep working with intentional breathing, you'll start a process that seems to have no limits. Your breath is your greatest ally. In any situation where you don't know what to do, simply return to your breath.

FOCUSED AWARENESS AND INNER VISUAL ACUITY

Resting our center of awareness on an idea, feeling, or even a location in the body naturally draws transformational energy to it. This awareness is a fiery energy that burns away layers of dross, body armor, and unconsciously held belief systems through compassionate self-acceptance and awareness. Our awareness can travel through and over our body using proprioception. The mental state is one of curious awareness and acceptance, witnessing what is simply there. While awareness, by itself, is healing and transformative, you have to stay focused on a spot, on a process, to move through it. Without focus, we just pop from one sensation to the next without any real movement forward.

Focused awareness can change shape by growing larger or smaller. It can also change quality, such as noticing a line of tension through your body. I imagine an inner spotlight that can shine on an area of the body and even into it. You can shift the focus of this spotlight to be rather small, like a laser beam, engaging a specific area of the body, like a spot of tension, or you can focus broadly, bringing awareness to a larger area, like a foot, a leg, the lower half of your body, or even your whole body all at once.

When we bring focused awareness to our experience it becomes more visual as well, like a magnifying glass looking through and revealing information about your body and your healing experience. I call this capacity your inner visual acuity. Over time, as you develop a capacity to keep your awareness focused on a stable experience, inner visual acuity becomes sharper, more clearly detailed, nuanced, and truly dynamic. It's like using a microscope to view the human body while simultaneously navigating a vast territory to be explored with adventures to encounter. It is both imaginal and higher dimensional in experience. What eye is it that you are actually looking with?

❦ Focused Awareness Exercise 1

Get to know your proprioceptive sense. Lying flat on your back, with eyes closed, begin to explore parts of your body using your inner spotlight. Bring your awareness only to one toe, then broaden the focus to the foot, both feet, then the bottom half of the body. Move your inner spotlight around the body in different sizes and notice how you can sense that location in the body. What happens if you hold it in one spot and breathe into it? What happens if you split the awareness across two locations? What does your inner visual acuity show you? Focus on a visual aspect of the experience and see what happens.

❦ Focused Awareness Exercise 2

Sit in meditation in front of a small table and light a candle that's about level with your eyes. Meditate on the candle. Start with a minute and every day go a little longer. Do the same with meditating on your third eye (the space between your eyebrows), your heart center, your belly, your hips and sacrum, and any spot of tension and remember to breathe into that spot. Focus on one of these areas and the candle at the same time. What happens?

Combining the use of the breath and your inner focus in this way corresponds to the element of fire and calcination, the first stage of alchemy. Most of the time, your breath and awareness are very gentle, a gentle circular breath with a gentle focus, rather than the burning intensity of a breathwork practice.

ALLOWING, ACCEPTING, AND RELAXING INTO (TRUSTING) THE PROCESS

As our awareness is developed, breath relaxes the physical body enough to accept the present moment and be curious about it, just as it is. From this state, a melting and dissolution occurs, allowing for release and healing.

Wherever the spotlight of awareness touches, a sense of deep relaxation naturally follows. This is a process that can be mindfully cultivated through intention and practice. As you witness an area in the body, using your proprioceptive sense, intend for the area to gently and naturally relax. The inner experience has a quality of letting go and surrendering, as the body tension dissolves and melts. There's no rushing, or doing, only allowing. Relaxing into an experience may also mean relaxing into tension or pain and simply letting it do what it needs to do (not trying to get rid of or avoid it, especially by moving the body). If the pain intensifies, which it will sometimes do, breathe deeper to help move it but most importantly, relax even more into the experience. These are called contractions and discharges. So paradoxically, relaxing and allowing may look like your body actively tensing up or shaking. This is good news. Keep going.

The energetic quality of this experience corresponds to dissolution, the second stage of alchemy, and the element of water. I imagine my tension being made of some sort of water-soluble material, like salt, and the edges gently being melted away as they're immersed in the compassionate and accepting water of my own consciousness. I use the breath to move the water, to keep it fresh, and to make more room for dissolved tension to leave the body.

❧ Relaxation Exercise 1

Get to know the experience of relaxing muscles and tension. Tighten all the muscles in your arms and hands. Hold for a few moments before letting go of this tension all at once. Notice the physical sensations of the transition between the moments of tension and relaxation. It has a quick dissolving or melting quality. After doing this a few times, begin to imagine that this sensation can be experienced on subtler and subtler levels, both lengthening the experience of the transition and allowing the body to enter deeper and deeper levels of relaxation. How far can you extend this experience? Another analogy is listening to the tone of a singing bowl trail off. The more relaxed we are, the longer we can hear it ring. Practice tightening and relaxing other parts of your body and then your whole body. Continue to explore the sensations of the transition.

Paradoxically, tension may be the door to the deepest relaxation. Some tensions can be relaxed quickly, but we begin to discover as we practice this that there are some areas of our body that constantly hold tension. When we engage these spaces actively, we can finally understand and let go of the root causes of the pain we experience.

❦ Relaxation Exercise 2

Lying down, get to know the subtle sense of muscle and tissue relaxation. Using your spotlight, bring your awareness to an area of tension. Apply the memory of the sensation of your experience of relaxation in "Relaxation Exercise 1" to this area of tension. Imagine this area of tension is a chunk of salt surrounded by crystal-clear water. Imagine the edges of the tension dissolving into the clear water. Continue to breathe into it.

❦ Relaxation Exercise 3

Practice using your breath and your proprioceptive sense to move the clear water holding the dissolved tension from the previous exercise through the channels in your body and out of your body. Usually, people imagine it exiting the feet, but it really could be anywhere. One time, I felt tension leave my body out of my left ear. It felt like a hose of air being blown out of it. You do this by imagining relaxing the body and opening the channels ahead of where you want this dissolved tension to go. This process may even cause spontaneous twitches, vibrations, or even shaking, especially when used in conjunction with psychedelic cannabis.

The capacities of focused awareness and deep relaxation represent a primary conjunction, or combination, of divergent elements central to these healing practices. As mentioned, they're symbolized by the alchemical elements of fire and water, respectively. The next two capacities—*understanding and discernment* and *curiosity, creativity, and play*—represent the other primary conjunction and are symbolized by the elements of air and earth, respectively.

UNDERSTANDING AND DISCERNMENT

Understanding naturally emerges from a deeper source in the self as we clear blockages that prevent us from experiencing our body in the present moment. This skill may come from study and be rational, but it comes from study that's applied again and again, and this is called *experience*. For example, any doctor with twenty years' experience as a physician has some sort of quality, even if it's hard to define, that makes them more skillful than a new, but brilliant, doctor. There's just something about repeating a task a thousand times. Discernment—the ability to distinguish one process from another, to *name* something as different from something else—comes from understanding and experience. Discernment is different from judgment in that it doesn't add a moral or a good/ bad quality to the awareness, and this is important. If you don't know what something is, you won't know how to work with it skillfully. Understanding is associated with the air element, the rational, mental quality, and the third stage of alchemy called separation.

❧ Understanding and Discernment Exercise I

Stay curious by naming your experience. As you experience different areas of your body using these practices, you may notice other sensations or awareness. One way to keep the mind from wandering and to stay focused is to name your experience as you're experiencing it. Physical sensations such as tension, pain, relaxation, and openness; energetic sensations such as warmth, coolness, buzzing, or whirling; and emotional experiences and mental thought processes including memories can seem to emerge from your body. Practice naming the emotions you're feeling and the thoughts that accompany them. Allow the sensations and feelings to be there, then look under them—what else is there? Let these experiences relax as you bring more and more awareness to relaxing the body.

❦ Understanding and Discernment Exercise 2

Practice naming different aspects of your present-moment experience during different journey experiences. Your naming can be very general or very specific. For example, go through your practice focusing only on physical sensations and naming them. Or focus only on emotions. The best way to find a great list of emotions and how they relate to each other is to search for the term *feeling wheel* online.

CURIOSITY, CREATIVITY, AND PLAY

The qualities of curiosity, creativity, and play are essential to any psychedelic healing experience. Playfulness is a powerful resource that can even be brought into the most difficult moments. There's a curiosity in playfulness, a desire to explore and to know, to see what else is there. Playfulness can bring magic to the psychedelic journey. Playfulness is a very present-moment experience but without agenda. Creativity is combined with the imagination as a form of authentic self-expression. These capacities are associated with the body, as well, the earth element in alchemy, and the fourth alchemical stage of conjunction. When we are healthy and vibrant, we are naturally curious, creative, and playful.

❦ Curiosity, Creativity, and Play Exercise 1

Bring a broad focused awareness to your entire body, take a few deep breaths, and relax. What do you notice most in your body? It may be a sensation or even a tension or pain. Take a breath with it. Notice what happens. Remain curious about the location in the body. Ask yourself, What's in here? What's underneath this sensation? Explore what's under it, then explore what's under that. Keep going, layer by layer. After a while, allow your awareness to rest again on your entire body and notice without attachment where your attention is drawn. You can explore different locations in the body or go deeper into a particular area. Let go of having an agenda and just play in your awareness.

❦ Curiosity, Creativity, and Play Exercise 2

Draw your experience using shapes, lines, textures, and colors. Once you're done, allow yourself to explore the images that arise again from your imagination as you look at your drawing. You can zoom into one spot and amplify it, taking another page to draw what you've seen more deeply. Keep going. What else is there, hidden deeper beneath the surface of the paper?

Combining the two elements of discernment and curiosity is a powerful practice. Understanding and discernment join together with curiosity, creativity, and play to build what we call creative problem-solving. Healing not only happens in our bodies but also in coming up with solutions to problems that matter to us in our lives. Problem-solving, in a sense, is a form of life healing and acknowledges the ecosystem we're embedded in. As we begin to resolve tensions in our bodies, we're naturally drawn toward solutions that, if implemented, would greatly impact our lives. This is another example of the holotropic nature of these practices.

The combination of all of these capacities with the power of the breath, the awareness of the body, and the sense of self *within* will build your experiences into a healthy and stable psychedelic practice. To work toward balance, use the guide below. The five inner capacities align well with our multiparadigm model, which includes the within. What areas of your personal practice are well developed, and what areas could use a little attention? Remember, these skill sets can be developed. Take your time and develop a practice that's sustainable, but expeditious enough to build from. Above all else, have fun with it.

We can again return to the words spoken in the Mindful Journeywork practice. Notice that these statements correspond to the

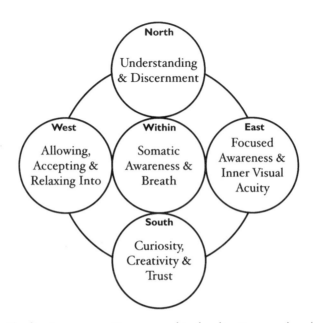

The five inner capacities mapped to the directions explored
in the Mindful Journeywork practice.

five inner capacities as well as the transpersonal dimensions of this work (called the vertical axis, above, below, and within) in the last three lines, representing the seven stages of transformational alchemy. Fundamentally, it's a practice of personal empowerment in alignment with the greatest good for all people and the planet.

The Mindful Journeywork Practice

I still myself and breathe.
I bring focused awareness to my present-moment experience.
I remain curious about sensations in my body and energetic field.
I feel fully and allow the inner journey to unfold all around me.
I discern my thoughts and harvest insight, understanding, and mastery.
I center in the support of my ancestors and of this sacred Earth.
I rise up to explore infinite possibility.
I manifest my calling in this life for the benefit of all beings.

22

Foundational Psychedelic Journeywork Practices

Getting started with any psychedelic practice can be quite intimidating. There are significant barriers to entry, the first of which is wanting to do it *right* and not knowing exactly how. I'm hoping this book is helping to break down some of those barriers, but at some point, you're just going to have to take a small step into the work, then another, and another, and another. I was going to say "take a leap" into the work, but things have changed. It used to be the case that you had to take that drink, or eat those mushrooms, or swallow the pill, and just go for it. That isn't the case anymore, and psychedelic cannabis is one way to ease in. You can safely and gently step into psychedelic cannabis practices that are deeply meaningful from the beginning and later deepen your practice when you're ready.

This next chapter outlines the general practices common to any psychedelic therapy or breathwork experience and how to gradually step into the work, especially if you've never done something like this before. Remember that the healing path of psychedelic cannabis is one of agency. What that means is healing and transformation at a pace and depth that you choose. When you're stepping into these practices, simply ask yourself what you're ready for. If you aren't sure, take a step back and choose a practice you know you can handle. Only go at a pace you're comfortable with and deepen your practices as you're ready to.

Again, a low dose of cannabis with some mindfulness practices is very safe. If you're not ready for that, just start with the mindfulness practices. And when you're ready, get to know the medicine. Take half a puff. Cannabis is by nature inherently helpful. Just take your time with it.

PREPARING TO WORK WITH CANNABIS

If you haven't worked with cannabis before, the whole process of getting started can be a bit anxiety provoking. It feels weird going into a dispensary for the first time because of decades of prohibition. Just know you're not the only person who feels this way. In fact, most do, and this feeling is part of what we're looking to heal. Don't let it get in the way of finding the medicine you need.

You will also need a nice vaporizer or a pipe. We use a specialized vaporizer in our practice because it can be temperature controlled, it works with the flower, and it's sturdy. I would recommend using a vaporizer over a pipe if you have never smoked cannabis before. If you choose a pipe, get one you feel you can use with intention. Maybe it's a bit ornate or larger than one you would normally use. There are some impressively beautiful pipes in the world. Find one that has meaning to you, and it will become more meaningful over time. Keep your pipe and medicine in a decorative container and only take it out for your journeywork sessions.

Getting Started

We've already talked about setting up a space, but really, in the beginning, just play some gentle music and make a nice spot on your couch. Load your pipe with a strain you want to start with and take one puff but no more. Sit in meditation with your eyes closed and breathe into your belly. Maybe that's enough for the first time, or maybe you want to go deeper. Take another puff at about the ten-minute mark, then pause again. Let this gentle experience be your first time.

Don't be surprised if even these small doses are stronger than you anticipated. Be ready to sit there for a little while. Give yourself space to enjoy it. You might experience very unusual sensations and maybe even the trembling or shaking form of discharge. But you can play in this space for as long as you want. You can start trying different strains, keeping notes, and experimenting with them in combination. This is how I worked with the plant for many years, and I still enjoy the method.

If you have a yoga or mindfulness practice already, you can incorporate these puffs of cannabis into your established practice. Notice how it impacts the practice. Maybe some strains aren't a great combination and interfere with the practice. Just remember that there are radically different strains to try out, as well. Keep a journal of your experiences and what you're learning. The medicine itself will begin to teach you through this process.

Remember, never drive after imbibing. That's your first rule: always stay safe and keep others safe in these practices.

Getting Bored

I encourage you to do these simple practices for as long as they serve you. But at some point, you might get bored. I would guess most mindfulness teachers would say to work with the boredom, to look under it, and to see what's there. Maybe you're avoiding something. I like to ask myself, "What am I not aware of?" and see what arises in my practice.

Boredom, however, isn't an indication that these practices aren't working, or that psychedelic cannabis isn't a real thing. Boredom is generally telling you you're ready to go deeper into your practice. And we can do that with psychedelics. Believe me when I say that when working an edge of healing and waking up, you definitely won't be bored!

When you're ready to deepen your practice, one method is to start paying attention to your setting. Maybe it's time to get off the couch or to set up a space specifically designed for the experience. Maybe it's time to smoke a little bit (or a lot) more.

There are a number of sitting practices that can be amplified by the intentional use of cannabis. Sitting practices are generally less intense than those performed lying down. You can experiment with larger doses in sitting practices before lying down, but at some point, I strongly encourage you to lie on your back for these experiences. There is something about having to hold yourself up that limits the potential of the psychedelic cannabis experience. It's way easier to fully let go if you're already supine, with your body and head supported. When you're ready, I'd like to invite you to begin the body scan practice on page 151. To best prepare for this practice, let's explore some important concepts related to meditation first.

STRATEGIES FOR SUCCESSFUL MEDITATION

Location of Meditation and Body Pose

These practices should be done in a quiet place where you won't be interrupted for the duration of the meditation session. Unless you intend to go to sleep immediately after the scan, do the practice in a space set up for meditation, either on a cushioned mat, a yoga mat, or a blanket on the floor. The firm support helps us stay alert. Some people put a small pillow under the base of the neck to open the airways in the throat. Some people like to be completely flat with no pillow. Thicker pillows or a bolster under the knees can help with low back pain. This isn't supposed to be an endurance test. Get comfortable and find what works for you.

Lying down, your hands can be held outward on the floor next to the hips, with the palms opened slightly. Your legs should always remain uncrossed. This is called Savasana in many yoga traditions. An alternative position for the hands can be resting palms down on your belly or your chest, or with one hand on your belly and the other on your chest.

Falling asleep may indicate you really needed to sleep, so let your-self rest and turn toward getting more sleep in general. You should be able to stay awake more easily as you go along. If you can't seem to break through to staying awake for twenty minutes, you might want to consider a more intense practice like the breathwork practice out-lined in the next chapter. You could also take a puff of an energetic sativa.

Use of Visualization and Imagination

Use visualization to help develop your inner senses. I imagine a spot-light of awareness slowly scanning the inside of my body as I bring my awareness to different areas. Other possibilities include visualizing your body slowly filling with warm light or healing water. Be creative.

Breath

Begin by taking several deep breaths into the belly. Belly breathing is one of the most important parts of the scan. Belly breathing makes the belly rise (while breathing in) and fall (when exhaling) while the chest remains mostly still or rises gently with the belly or after the breath fills it. The breath should be gentle, intentional, and have depth but also be relaxed and not forced or too strong. You don't need fill up your lungs to their greatest capacity or exhale them until they're completely empty. Breathe into what's comfortable but nudge up against the edges of your breath.

Circular breathing is gently breathing into the belly without paus-ing at the top or bottom of the breath. This means you'll immedi-ately begin to exhale after you inhale, and then begin to inhale just as you finish your exhale. There aren't any long pauses between breaths or holding. Don't push the air out of your lungs, just let go naturally.

After watching so many people over the years doing this practice, I've found that it is one of the most effective breathing techniques for the body scan practice as well as psychedelic journeywork. With each breath, you're exploring the edges of cultivating and growing with the inhale and the deep letting go of the exhale, over and over again. This technique also seems to represent the breath of a healthy, resting nervous system. Because breath also helps us move and amplify energy, circular breathing will amplify any psychedelic experience. Slowing down your breathing will deepen relaxation but may stall your inner process. Never stop breathing in the body scan practice. Stay with the gentle, circular breathing. If at any time you lose track of where you are in the scan, go back to the awareness of your breath before continuing on from where you remember last being in your body.

You can amplify your relaxation practice of the body scan by imagining you're filling up the area you're focusing on in the scan with your breath. This is described as breathing into a location in your body, breathing into a memory, or even breathing into an emotional experience. For the body, breathing is equated with acceptance, which allows for the healing of difficult emotional experiences.

As you bring your awareness to an area of your body, imagine your breath also going fully into that area. A consequence of bringing awareness and breath to these locations is to relax them naturally. You don't have to *do* anything else. Just resting your awareness on an area, breathing into it, and choosing to relax there is enough.

Gentle Stillness

Staying with an area long enough to relax it requires focused attention. Moving your body to adjust something that feels uncomfortable can shut down the process. Therefore, I would like to invite you to explore gentle stillness. Gentle stillness is the intention to ignore the instinct to move to adjust a tension in your body once you get settled or to move in other deliberate ways. This allows for a deepening of the experience. The mind is fully engaged in proprioception—again, our ability to sense parts of our body and how much tension we hold there, allowing us to become aware of and relax tension in the body. Of course, be gentle with yourself. This is not an endurance test.

However, something about gentle stillness allows psychedelic cannabis to amplify significantly.

You may begin to experience unusual sensations, such as tingling and warmth, or small muscle contractions and spasms, emotional releases, memories, and thoughts. Letting these happen and *relaxing into them* is all that's required. This is also gentle stillness; letting yourself spontaneously twitch, tremble, and shake is an important part of the healing process.

Again, resist the urge to move to alleviate discomfort around these sensations, especially small discomforts like itches and other unusual tensions. They'll pass, and something really important is usually resting right under them. It helps to imagine that these sensations are simply the tensions leaving the body, the discharge of a symptom, as described earlier. This allows us to relax into discomfort because we know this is what healing actually looks and feels like. It's okay to step back from an intense experience and take a break from it by resting your awareness on a wider perspective of that area or somewhere else completely.

Gentle circular breathing and gentle stillness provide a foundation not only for profound psychedelic cannabis experiences but for the amplification of any psychedelic experience.

THE BODY SCAN

The body scan meditation is a central component of the Captain Protocol. It is the practice of systematically scanning the body for tension and relaxing those areas and is the foundational mindfulness practice for the Medicinal Mindfulness program. The body scan helps develop the inner capacities outlined in chapter 21 that are useful tools for psychedelic journeywork and guide work, such as increasing your awareness of your body and inner processes. The body scan meditation combines the development of these five capacities into one integrated practice and is essential in clearing and healing deeply held physical, psychological, and spiritual tensions and traumas. It is this dual purpose that makes it such an important process. It cultivates capacities we want to develop while simultaneously helping us clear what no longer serves us.

The body scan meditation is a very common practice, and there are many ways to work with it. There is a recorded body scan meditation on the Medicinal Mindfulness website under the Media tab. There are a few versions, and they're specifically designed to be incorporated into psychedelic journeywork music sets.

Again, if you're new to working with either cannabis or mindfulness practices, I'd recommend starting the scan in a sober state. This is something I recommend my clients and students do on a regular basis without cannabis. Having some sort of mindfulness or yogic practice without cannabis, anyway, helps you increase your skill sets in these areas. You can work at a pace appropriate for you, but it should be at least once a week for any meaningful progress. Three times a week would be considered a lot for most people; however, the body scan can be as short as fifteen to twenty minutes.

Again, this is the foundation of a psychedelic cannabis experience with the intention of working to heal and wake up. The body scan is generally facilitated at the beginning of any psychedelic cannabis experience. I'm going to describe the basics of it here so you can start practicing, but after the next chapter on how to facilitate your own psychedelic cannabis sessions, we're going to circle back to the body scan on a whole other level by working with the Five Awareness Practice and another practice called tracking. These practices work off of the solid foundation of the body scan, so don't skip the body scan if you've already done it before. That would be like me saying I don't need to do push-ups if I want to build my strength because I've already done one before.

These important foundational practices amplify psychedelic states by helping you orient to the primary ways we perceive and sense our inner experience. They provide a way to discern and deepen our process.

The body scan, in general, is a wonderful way to prepare for psychedelic experiences. Just like any exercise, doing it more often improves the results. Set a goal that's realistic for you and meet it.

Resources

Use the Body Scan Record Sheet in the appendix at the back of this book as a model to bring more intention and structure to your practice. It's sometimes helpful to see progress over a period of time.

While I recommend you practice guiding yourself with the scan to help develop your capacity to focus, this is a difficult practice to start on your own. The recorded guided meditations are a great way to get started.

Order of the Body Scan

Use the order below as an initial guide. Begin the scan at your feet and gradually move up the body as follows:

- Toes, feet, ankles
- Shins and calves
- Knees, thighs, pelvis, and hips
- Genitals, lower abdomen, and lower back
- Organs of the abdomen
- Mid-back and diaphragm
- Muscles and ribs of the chest and upper back
- Organs of the chest, lungs, and heart
- Shoulders and shoulder blades
- Tops and sides of shoulders
- Down the arms and into the elbows, forearms, wrists, hands, and fingers
- Back to the throat and base of the neck
- Sides of the neck and base of the skull, the jaw, the muscles around the mouth, nose, eyes, ears, forehead
- Sides and back of head, top of head, brain, then the energetic field

- Relax the emotions in the heart and memories, thoughts, and judgments in the head.

When being guided, either in person or by a meditation track, you simply follow the voice of the person guiding you. When guiding yourself, you can be more specific or more general, move up and then down the body, or up the body several times. Practice in a way that works for you. Use your imagination. There is no one right way to do this.

Movement, Stretching, and Self-Massage with a Body Scan

Cannabis significantly amplifies our somatic awareness while simultaneously supporting the relaxation of deeply held tensions in the body. These simple traits are foundational to somatic trauma resolution. Now that I've shared that gentle stillness is probably the most important factor in these experiences and strongly encouraged you to practice gentle stillness and breath regularly, I would like to invite you to explore the opposite: intentional movement. Stretching while using cannabis was a practice developed thousands of years ago. Practices like yoga were developed with the support of cannabis in many traditions.

In these initial, even lower-dose sessions, you might find you want to spontaneously move and stretch areas of your body, and that it feels really good to do so. If you're trained in yoga, practice yoga, but also take some time to let your movement and stretches be guided by your body and your intuition.

It is possible to hurt yourself if you go too quickly or too deep into your stretching. The goal is to gently hold the edges of what's comfortable and breathe into the sensation. Try releasing and stretching into the same spaces gently with your breath. Don't try to push through tension or pop joints or other things. That isn't the point of it. Gently find the edges of what's comfortable, rock back and forth into it very gently and breathe, or move slowly from side to side. Give yourself plenty of space to do these practices. There are spaces in psychedelic journeywork that support trauma healing through the spontaneous movement of the body, and sometimes it can look like stretching in very unusual positions. Trust the wisdom of the body, breathe with it, and go slowly.

Self-massage is another practice often helpful in releasing significant tension from the body. There are important areas that can be reached with your own hands. These areas include tension points in the chest and sternum, tension in the upper belly and around the diaphragm and ribs, and also the lower belly. Some spots might be quite tender. Gently exploring the body and addressing knots and points of tension is a useful and necessary tool for self-healing. Again, as with stretching, massaging too hard is also possible. Find the edges of what you can handle and stay there, often taking time to release the massage so a muscle can rest. Again, cannabis amplifies this process.

To work on your back, shoulders, neck, hips, and so forth, consider getting massage tools like a massage hook, golf balls for the feet, tennis balls and larger massage balls for the thighs and hips, and foam rollers to rest on. These are amazing tools for self-healing, but they're not required in the beginning if you want to get started without them. Again, go slowly. Find your limits, breathe into them, and relax. Don't try to push yourself over your edges.

After any movement series, you are strongly encouraged to lie down and practice gentle stillness. Reengage the body scan throughout your body.

Typical Body Scan and Movement Sessions

A typical body scan session lasting twenty minutes to about an hour and a half looks something like this:

1. Space preparation and music setup
2. Optional imbibing ceremony (a few puffs to a full series): 10 minutes
3. Lying down (supine) body scan practice: 10 to 20 minutes
4. Optional gentle music set: 30 to 60 minutes
5. Gentle returning: 10 minutes

A typical movement session lasting one to two hours can look something like this:

1. Space preparation and music setup
2. Optional imbibing ceremony (a few puffs to a full series): 10 minutes
3. Optional lying down (supine) body scan practice (or skip this and proceed immediately into gentle stretching): 10 to 20 minutes
4. A set of gentle intuitive movement and stretching practices: 30 to 60 minutes
5. Lying down (supine) body scan practice: 10 to 20 minutes
6. Gentle returning: 10 minutes

Sessions like these may or may not be psychedelic. It will mostly depend on how much medicine you take and the quality of the blend. Don't underestimate the transformational nature of these practices. Over time, they can make a big difference. Remember, if you get bored, it doesn't mean it is not working or that you're doing something wrong. It is just time to take it to the next level. Remember to breathe into your belly and to practice gentle stillness.

Other Ways to Use
the Body Scan Practices

This family of body scan practices can also be explored with a friend or small group. They provide a wonderful way to share in a sacred healing experience, to reduce risk, and to increase a sense of safety. Most of these practices, however, are internal, so make sure there is plenty of time to turn inward, even if you're working with others.

You can also combine the body scan meditation (the option above without the extra music at end) with other tracks that will create a gentle journey experience that fits within the time frame above. Instead of trying to keep track of the time, let the music keep track for you. Certain songs may denote switching to the next stage of the practice.

23

Psychedelic Cannabis and Breathwork Practices

Now that we've explored the foundational practices, let's take a look at the primary psychedelic journeywork practices specifically designed to best facilitate psychedelic cannabis experiences.

There are two primary internal processes you're going to be working with. The first is most closely aligned with healing trauma, releasing dross, and letting go of tensions and psychological states that don't serve you. The second, a spontaneous process you're going to experience, is a deeper relationship with yourself and the deep meanings you wish to cultivate and live into. Both, in a sense, are processes of becoming even more of who you are.

Psychedelic cannabis seems to be specifically made to facilitate this process in a way that feels more grounding and in the body than other psychedelics. It is a wonderful tool to help integrate other psychedelic medicines, but it's also its own powerful practice. In some ways, healing and self-actualization might simply be different locations on the same continuum of development. To heal, we must wake up, and to fully awaken, we must heal. In other words, they might be one and the same: healing-awakening.

The following practices are options for your healing-awakening process. Once you feel comfortable with the blends you've been exploring, the body scan, and other practices, you're invited to step into the deep waters of healing and transformation. Remember that safety is your number one priority, and there's no reason to do these practices in a way that feels unsafe. You can always start light with the medicine and take more as needed. The practices themselves build on each other and are part of the Captain Protocol as skill development and resilience development practices. They're also a lot of fun. Give yourself permission to experiment with and explore the inner landscapes created by these experiences. First, we'll explore the psychedelic cannabis practices, then the noncannabis breathwork practices, then finally the cannabis-assisted breathwork practices. I'm not sharing this information with the expectation that you'll go as deeply as humanly possible but to let you know you can always go deeper if you want to or are ready to.

All of these practices have the same general space requirements and general setup. They're just different strategies for healing and awakening.

THE PSYCHEDELIC CANNABIS HEALING-AWAKENING PRACTICE

Psychedelic cannabis experiences are generally three to five hours in length, with one to two psychedelic cannabis sets about an hour and a half long each, with a break in the middle for the two-set practice. Generally, the first stage of the session includes a personal check-in, such as a meditation practice, journaling, and setting an intention. Giving yourself plenty of time afterward is equally important, especially in the beginning when you're still learning how the medicine affects you. For new cannabis users, sometimes one set is plenty and can last a little longer, perhaps an hour and a half to two hours in length. The key to the duration is the intensity of the medicine. If you're starting to get bored or sleepy, you might be coming down. Either allow yourself to come down by gently stretching the body and slowly returning or take a moment and smoke more of the medicine.

After you set an intention and are ready to imbibe, take a quick bathroom break so your bladder doesn't pull you out of the experience too soon. The cannabis is then imbibed with intention, usually through a guided meditation or the gratitude prayer. Most are ready to lie down and begin the body scan meditation at this time. Remember to fade your music into the body scan meditation if you're using a recorded meditation, or to the music you wish to listen to during your own scan. Sometimes it takes a little while to adjust to the psychedelic cannabis space, so you can remain sitting up if you'd like or gently stretch a few minutes before lying down. Before you lie down, check in with your intuition and body to see if you should take more of the medicine.

Sometimes when you lie down after smoking a significant amount of psychedelic cannabis in a very short period of time, it can feel like taking off in a rocket ship. Your body might feel incredibly unusual, your heart might race, and your anxiety might increase. Stay in contact with your gentle breathing and relax around the experience. It doesn't last that long, and your body, including your heart rate and respiration, will become more manageable. Remember that you have the nano-encapsulated CBD if the experience feels too intense.

If your session is longer with two sets, create a music set with a song you'll recognize as the intermission and check in with yourself to see if you need a bathroom break or more medicine. You can also take a moment to stretch and journal a little before taking the second dose of the medicine. If you want to go deeper, you can smoke as much as you did in the first set, or you can keep the process going at about the same level if you smoke a little more than half as much. Some people just take a toke or two to elevate the experience slightly.

At the end of the experience, have a song ready to denote the completion of the session and gently allow yourself to come back if you're ready to do so. Depending on how you set up the session, you can keep the music going for a long return or intentionally pull yourself out of the experience by slowly beginning to move and stretch.

During this period, I imagine I'm breathing myself back into a cohesive form. With every breath, I imagine I'm consolidating my light body into a healthy and vibrant matrix of light. It's important you take the time to come all the way back and to not return too abruptly. Once you're sitting back up and reorienting, have some juice or snacks, journal, use the restroom, and wash your face and hands. You'll feel like you've been through an unusual workout, especially if you trembled a lot. Make sure you drink plenty of water.

We'll discuss what you're actually doing in the session in the next chapter but generally speaking, simply focusing your awareness on an area of the body under the influence of psychedelic cannabis and staying with the experience for many minutes begins to transform that area automatically toward health. I bring an awareness of compassionate, accepting curiosity and ask often, What else is there? Usually, it takes only a few moments of guiding myself before the journey has a momentum all its own. At that point, we simply support the unfolding or unwinding through focused awareness and compassionate self-acceptance. When I'm going through a big process, I often remind myself that everything is okay with phrases like "This is what healing looks like," "Your body knows exactly what to do," "Trust your body, trust your breath," and "All is well."

Potential Paths of a Journey

A psychedelic cannabis journey can take many paths. Here are a few of the possibilities:

Typical journey—Imbibe, lie down, do a body scan, listen to a music set, and have an inner journey experience

Resistance to lying down—If you find that you're feeling resistant to lying down, check in with yourself. Maybe do some gentle stretching first. If there is an opening to go inward, guide yourself to a supine position with a shorter body scan practice and keep your primary focus on a gentle, deep breath in the belly.

Immediate experience—If you immediately feel yourself going into an experience (you have muscular cramps or a process begins immediately), skip the body scan and just go right in. If this process resolves, return to the body scan if you like.

Immediate crisis or big release after smoking—An immediate crisis such as screaming or strong shaking may occur. Support yourself however necessary, keep yourself safe from injury, and let the process resolve. Remember that you have the nano-encapsulated CBD as an antidote if you need it.

Breathwork inclusion—Adding breathwork can be good for people who are stuck. You may be nervous to begin the breathwork practice, so shorten the body scan. Breathwork usually requires additional coaching because cannabis makes it more difficult to concentrate and exert breath. This is a special practice that requires an orientation before beginning.

Listed below are sample outlines for one- and two-set psychedelic cannabis sessions.

Sample Outline of a One-Set Psychedelic Cannabis Session (2 to 3 hours)

- Preliminary space setup and music prep
- Intention-setting, journaling, stretching: 20 to 30 minutes
- Bathroom break and pipe preparation: 10 minutes
- Imbibing ceremony: 10 minutes
- Guided body scan meditation: 15 to 20 minutes
- Music set: 60 to 75 minutes
- Returning guided meditation: 10 to 15 minutes
- Snacks, self-care, journaling, art, integration, closing: 30 to 45 minutes
- Resting, integrating, cleaning space

Sample Outline of a Two-Set Psychedelic Cannabis Session (3 to 5 hours)

- Preliminary space setup and music prep
- Intention-setting, journaling, stretching: 20 to 30 minutes

- Bathroom break and pipe preparation: 10 minutes
- Imbibing ceremony: 10 minutes
- Guided body scan meditation: 15 to 20 minutes
- First music set: 60 to 75 minutes
- Bathroom, smoking, and stretching break: 15 to 20 minutes
- Second music set (the average music set here is about 60 to 75 minutes in length): 75 to 90 minutes
- Returning guided meditation: 10 to 15 minutes
- Snacks, self-care, journaling, art, integration, closing: 30 to 45 minutes
- Resting, integrating, cleaning space

Tips for Psychedelic Cannabis Sessions

- Review the safety self-assessment and determine safety requirements.
- Set up a safe, contained space.
- Have a small trash can with a liner handy in case you need to vomit.
- High doses, concentrates, dabbing, and hash are not recommended or required.
- After imbibing with intention, lie down in a gentle, still, and open pose and wear an eye covering.
- Experiment with different types of music—use what works for you.
- Practice the body scan and tracking (as explained in the next chapter) and other skill set development practices.
- Have fun and enjoy the experience.
- Remember to be body and breath focused, particularly in the beginning.
- Have nano-encapsulated CBD as an antidote available.
- Start light and work your way to higher and higher states of awareness.

THE BREATHWORK
HEALING-AWAKENING PRACTICE

Breath is synonymous with life and spirit. It is not my intention to go fully into the theory of breathwork here, but there are a few things I would like to share with you before we get started. Physiologically speaking, breathwork practices increase the CO_2 levels in your circulatory system. It's a common misunderstanding that because you're going to be breathing more intensely, these practices oxygenate the blood. That simply isn't true from my understanding. While there are a lot of wonderful theories out there about how these practices work, like increasing your vital chi energy to amplify your healing process, I would like to share two theories that are starting to emerge through my own exploration.

One theory suggests that the increased level of CO_2 in the blood tricks the brain into thinking you're dying (when you're not at all coming even close). New scientific studies are showing that DMT is produced in the lungs and might activate when CO_2 reaches a certain level in the blood. When someone is literally dying, their breathing stops, so CO_2 levels naturally start to rise. Production of DMT, the proverbial spirit molecule, happens, according to Dr. Rick Strassman, because DMT helps the body and mind transition through death. This is why we see spirits and the white light when we die. We're having some sort of endogenous DMT release.

The second theory I've heard is that this form of breathwork, called circular breathing, which I introduced in the previous chapter, activates the autonomic nervous system of the body, both the sympathetic, which is activating, and the parasympathetic, which is a deep resting and healing space. Somehow, both of these elicit healing by activating trauma in a safe environment. I wasn't so sure about this idea as I didn't fully understand the science behind it. This changed one afternoon when I was holding my infant daughter to put her down for a nap. When she fell asleep, she started to naturally engage a gentler pattern of circular breathing similar to the one we use in these practices. At that moment, I had an intuitive realization that this was the same healing breath. The breathwork practice is an amplified version of the respiration of a deeply cared-for infant in a perfectly relaxed state of being.

I like to combine these two ideas to explain the experience. A spontaneous DMT release, as well as the corrective healing power of the autonomic nervous systems, are both greatly influencing the breathwork experience. This is the closest I can get to describing what's actually happening in the breathwork experience in any meaningful way.

The intensity of the breath isn't as important as the circular breathing. I've seen incredible healing states using gentle breathing practices. That said, I would encourage you to find the edges of your most intense breathing.

Engaging the breath is one of the most complex and powerful tools in psychedelic journeywork. It's also the simplest and most overlooked. We all have a right to use our own inner resources for healing. For that reason, access to breathwork is fundamentally a social justice issue. It's safe. And it's free. Other practitioners may disagree with the decision to share this information in this way. I personally view this from a harm reduction perspective and a social justice perspective. Healing trauma is generally safer than not healing it, and not everyone has access to legitimate breathwork facilitators or the training. We all have a fundamental right to use our own breath for healing purposes. Most of us just don't know how to do it.

Breathwork practices can be a little wild. Safety is your priority. Have a peer-sitter if you can and don't take unnecessary risks. Your peer-sitter is going to be there just to make sure you don't shake off the mat and into a corner or something and hurt yourself. I've done plenty of solo breathwork and have never felt unsafe in the experience, but I also took extra care in setting up the space.

While breathwork is safe, it's easy to underestimate the power of breathwork as a practice. It's regularly described in our circles as some of the most intense psychedelic experiences participants have ever had.

You can always titrate the breathwork practice to a level that feels manageable to you.

You'll also always want to engage in this practice on the floor, with a lot of space around you. You don't want to shake off your bed and hurt yourself. You can always start with a lighter breath or a gentle circular breathing with a body scan before doing a full breathwork practice. Get to know the practice just as you're getting to learn the spirit of cannabis.

The practice itself is very simple. Set up your space the same way you would for the other practices. You'll be breathing in and out of your mouth for the first forty-five minutes or so. The music will be more rhythmic and evocative for the first set, which is the breathwork practice, then it relaxes into more ethereal music for the last thirty minutes. You can also set the music to certain songs that intensify in the first set and mark the time at about five minutes, ten minutes, twenty minutes, and thirty minutes till the forty-five minute mark. These marks are an invitation to increase the intensity and depth of your breathing.

The breathing practice is pretty simple. You'll start out on the lighter side and try to increase the intensity of your breathing as you go, but the breath practice itself is similar throughout the first forty-five minutes. You'll be engaging in circular breathing through your mouth. Unlike holotropic breathwork, which is an intense inhale and an intense exhale similar to hyperventilating, this circular breathing is a pronounced inhale and a gentle letting go on the exhale. You don't want to slow your breathing down or push it out, just release the muscles in your diaphragm and let your body naturally relax and exhale. As the circular breath implies, you're going to take in another big breath just before completing the exhale and let it go immediately at the top. There's no holding or pausing the breath at the inhale or exhale. It's a continual rhythm of breathing with no pauses. Choose a series of songs that increase in rhythmic intensity and have them transition at about the 5-minute, 10-minute, 20-minute, and 35-minute marks to cue you to amplify your breathing practice at these times without having to look at a clock. This allows for a pacing in the practice that is physically sustainable.

At the different marks in the music, you're invited to amplify your breathing to the next level of intensity and continue to do so until something unusual happens. At some point, the autonomic nervous system kicks in, and your body starts breathing in this intense way without you having any conscious control over it. One of my teachers called this "the breath breathing you." It can be a very strange experience, and the body can breathe any number of ways at this time, from very fast and shallow to screaming breaths from deep within your soul. These are amazing and very healing experiences. Just like with the cannabis experience, you don't necessarily lose control, and you keep your agency. You're continually choosing to let go of control and trust the process. At any time, even when your breath is breathing you, you can start to shut down the process. But it's better not to; it's better to ride out the waves of the breath and to explore and even amplify the process. This is your body and your breath. Even if it's extremely intense, this may be what the body looks like in a natural and safe healing process.

Breathwork experiences are usually much louder than typical psychedelic cannabis experiences. Some people vocalize with their breath, or cry or laugh or scream and shout. Do it in a safe and private space so you can feel comfortable and unobserved. Feeling extreme emotions as they break free from your body and spirit is not uncommon.

At about the forty-five-minute mark, the music should shift to something gentle and relaxing. This is your cue to let the breath slowly start returning to normal as you surf the psychedelic state that the breathing induced.

Breathwork experiences can be extremely intense and even shocking. You should expect everything you experience on any psychedelic trip, but your body awareness is going to amplify to an extreme degree, as your body starts to release what it's holding in very unusual ways. It can feel like you're breaking out of chains or even concrete. This isn't a subtle process. Your hands, feet, and even the muscles around your mouth might tighten and cramp in a process called tetany. Although intense, it is a normal and temporary experience that doesn't harm the body. At this point, you have a choice to either back off of the breathing just a bit to make the sensations in your body more manageable or to breathe even more intensely and break through the pain of the experience. Both paths inevitably lead to healing. This is what healing looks like on your terms. You can choose to breathe intensely or gently. Either way, you're on a path to healing and awakening. You may wish to follow an outline such as the one below.

Sample Outline of a Breathwork Experience

- Preparation and room safety, cleaning and clearing, journey music preparation
- Intention setting
- Sacred space setting
- Brief body scan
- Breathwork practice: 45 minutes of evocative, rhythmic music. Music shifts (to something more evocative) at the 5-minute, 10-minute, 20-minute, and 35-minute marks
- Journey with gentle music for 30 to 45 minutes with resting breath and inner exploration
- Closing and returning
- Integration practices and self-care

Breathwork is a very simple, yet incredibly powerful psychedelic healing practice. There are some amazing communities devoted to a huge family of similar breathwork practices. If they're available to you, I strongly encourage you to check them out. This is the breathwork practice stripped down to its most essential form, without any particular metaphysics attached to it. While it can be intimidating to start a breathwork practice on your own, this is all you need to know to get started and develop a practice. I have seen incredible healing using the breath.

THE CANNABIS-ASSISTED BREATHWORK HEALING-AWAKENING PRACTICE

We have just discussed two simple but life-transforming tools you can learn to do on your own for healing and awakening. But what happens if we combine them? I've done so on my own several times, and some of them were the most healing practices I had ever engaged in. That didn't make them easy, but the combination of cannabis and breathwork provided fully somatic and psychedelic states that were some of the highest I'd ever reached. The first time we tried a cannabis-assisted breathwork session in a group, I was facilitating for a special event for students from my program. We had a circle of about twenty people and a band for live music. People were popping, not in a bad way, but in a way we hadn't expected. It appeared more like a 5-MeO-DMT experience than any breathwork experience I'd ever seen. All in all, it was amazing.

PSYCHEDELIC CANNABIS BREATHWORK BLEND

I recommend changing up the psychedelic cannabis blend because the Alchemy Blend might actually be too strong. I combine a medium sativa for energy with strains that the budtenders say people use for alleviating pain. I also add some CBN strains, and about a third of the blend is a high-potency CBD strain. This helps the body relax when it's contracting and experiencing tetany.

The breathing cycle is also radically different. Stay with the breath for as long as you can, even pushing yourself for the first fifteen minutes or so, but you might find that you drift from the breathwork practice at times and lose touch with your body awareness completely. If you return to your body awareness during the first part of the set, you're encouraged to keep breathing. I've seen some people drift in and out of the breathwork practice every ten minutes or so, and I've seen some people breathe intensely for an hour and a half. Therefore, until you really get to know the practice, I'd encourage you to give yourself a lot of room within the session to recover and drink plenty of water. Follow the outline below.

Sample Outline of a Cannabis-Assisted Breathwork Experience (three to five hours)

- Preparation and room safety, cleaning and clearing, journey music preparation
- Intention setting
- Imbibing ceremony
- Brief body scan
- Breathwork practice: 45 minutes of evocative, rhythmic music interspersed with gentler music. The music should still be rhythmic and increase in intensity before it shifts.
- Journey with gentler music interspersed with evocative music for another 45 to 60 minutes with resting breath and inner exploration. It'll take this long to come back enough to smoke again, but take a break when you're ready. This can be the completion of the practice or you can take a break and then start a second music set.
- Bathroom, smoking, and stretching break: 15 to 20 minutes
- Second music set: 75 to 90 minutes
- Returning guided meditation: 10 to 15 minutes
- Snacks, self-care, journaling, art, integration, closing: 30 to 45 minutes
- Closing and returning
- Integration practices and self-care

HEALING AND RESILIENCE

Ongoing Practices within the Captain Protocol

These beginner journeywork practices, psychedelic cannabis sessions, breathwork sessions, and even the cannabis-assisted breathwork sessions can be integrated into an ongoing practice that not only heals our trauma but simultaneously increases our resilience in life and personal empowerment.

The ongoing practices have a broad range of possibility. As I've noted, take your time with it and only do what you feel comfortable doing. If you're bored, then maybe it's an indication to go deeper into the practices by increasing your dose, amplifying your process with your breath, or turning toward creating a space that feels even more safe and contained. I've seen people practice this in sets of sessions, with significant amounts of time in between, and I've also seen people set a weekly schedule of regular practices. Set a schedule that works for you. Repeat and experiment with the practices until you find the ones you like, you reach the desired outcome, and you establish a pace that works for you.

Interestingly, psychedelic cannabis experiences can also be an important integration tool for other psychedelic medicine experiences, such as an ayahuasca retreat. I have observed often that most psychedelic journeys have incomplete threads, and while a person could benefit from another psychedelic experience, it would be too much or come too soon. I call this the remaining 10 percent. Cannabis can be a great tool in these situations because it allows the journeyer to tap back into that deep psychedelic state to complete the last 10 percent within a much shorter and less physically demanding session. We'll discuss additional tools for ongoing support and healing in part 5.

24

Tracking and the Five Awareness Practice

Because cannabis provides a sense of agency, sometimes difficult experiences don't automatically activate as they do in other psychedelic medicine experiences, and instead we're required to take active steps toward them for healing to take place. All of the chapters so far are like pieces to a complex puzzle that initiates the healing process. But what do we do in the psychedelic cannabis process itself to further facilitate healing and awakening?

TRACKING

Just as a hunter tracks an animal in the forest, following clues to where it is, so too can the psychedelic journeyer track their inner experience to follow clues to deeper awareness and healing processes. After we practice the body scan for a period of time, we begin to notice there are subtler experiences hidden deep within the physical body that often don't shift much with the scan. The experiences may seem more stable, or they may feel so set in place that they won't relax anymore. They may even feel like a pain or kinks in our joints or muscles that you begin to realize have been there for a very long time. In the extreme, these are the source points for much more intense and debilitating pains or even chronic illness.

I describe these sensations as the subtle tensions because they're hidden by the gross day-to-day tensions and activities of our bodies. We all have that spot where we store things we don't want to look at. Those memories begin to accumulate in that location of the body and create a block in the channel and a physical kink in our fascia. This is what Wilhelm Reich termed *body armor,* and what we call dross, as mentioned earlier.

The simple practice of tracking takes the body scan to an intuitive, open level, so it is not just systematically visiting and relaxing each location in the body but following what you most notice in the body, mind, and emotions as it arises. This practice supports the holotropic nature of the human body and psyche to move toward wholeness by relaxing around it and allowing it to happen without resistance. Even though the practitioner is generally very still throughout the process, it's a very active and internally rich state of awareness.

The way to practice tracking is to take a breath and turn toward what you most notice in your body, whatever and wherever it is. Take another breath and repeat. Over time, the sensations change so you track the changes in your awareness. The mantra we use is: "Bring awareness to my body, use my breath to surrender." Repeat again and again and again.

In any given moment, what are you most aware of in your body? Rest in that awareness. Breathe with it. And then repeat. In the next moment, what are you most aware of in your body? This is usually a strong somatic sensation, tension, or pain. Rest in that awareness. Breathe with it. This process is repeated with each breath, and the changes in the sensations are followed using the five inner capacities.

As you do this, you may realize that what you notice begins to move and what you're most aware of in one moment isn't what you were aware of a moment ago. And if you consider it, what you repeatedly become aware of in succession makes a path that can be followed to deeper experiences and understanding.

Engage your five inner capacities in this practice. Breath is the spirit that heats the crucible of transformation (your body). Focused awareness corresponds to the first stage of alchemy, the fire and heat that burns through the dross and helps release it. Surrender corresponds to the second stage of alchemy, dissolution and water, which dissolves the chunks of dross we release during the first process.

This is the mechanism of the inner radar and inner healing intelligence that specifically guides us toward what's most ready to heal, develop, or transform. If we learn to allow this process, our bodies and psyches naturally move toward wholeness. Tracking facilitates this process.

This is quite simple in theory but is often difficult to do, especially when the material touches on what we'd rather not look at. According to this model, however, awareness is healing in and of itself, and healing occurs when we allow a symptom, which is defined as anything we're experiencing, an opportunity to move through and out of our body. Tracking is following the present moment experience of this occurrence and facilitating it by not resisting it, accepting that it's happening, and allowing it to pass.

Listed below are a number of more advanced techniques:

- **Tracking deeper into a location**—Instead of scanning the body, or after scanning the body, hold your awareness on one area of the body for an extended period of time. Allow yourself to witness what's there and relax deeper and deeper into the experience of that location. Significant places to explore are any areas of tension or pain, the stomach, the heart, and the eyes.
- **Naming multiple, simultaneous experiences**—As you explore an area of the body with the body scan and tracking, allow your awareness to hold multiple layers of the experience/sensation simultaneously. Start with energetic and physical sensations. Then name emotional content. Then allow the awareness to witness any thought processes or memories. Take time to name the different qualities of the experiences and begin to develop a vocabulary for subtle physical and energetic sensations, discharges, or complex emotions.
- **Tracking nonlinearly through the body**—As we hold our awareness over an area of tension, we can often experience movements and sensations throughout our body discharging simultaneously or seemingly randomly. We first feel something in the

shoulder, then a spot in the back, then in the neck, then the legs, then back to the shoulder, and so on. Simply tracking the experience as it happens and gently holding your awareness of the sensation until you notice something else is the point of tracking. When we simply let our body unwind in our own compassionate awareness, deep healing and new understandings naturally occur, unfolding into conscious awareness.

- **Burning through a blockage**—Use the heat of your focused awareness to burn through blockages by focusing like a magnifying glass on the most intense/painful part. Use the water of surrender to relax around these spaces and clear any loosened dross.
- **Filling a void space**—What do you not notice in your body? Sometimes areas of deep pain are hidden beneath a sheath of invisibility. Get to know these spaces by learning their contours. Fill them with self-compassion, love, and acceptance.
- **External tracking**—Bring the awareness of the body scan and tracking into your daily life. Take a few moments to check in with your inner awareness of your body and witness what's there. Make note of areas of tension, breathing into them and bringing your spotlight and sense of relaxation to them. Check in during times of stress but also during times of joy. What do you notice? How can you use the information your body is giving you? Do this as often as you remember to.

THE FIVE AWARENESS PRACTICE

Becoming conscious of how we sense and perceive in nonordinary states allows us to better orient to, engage in, and understand the transpersonal experience. The five basic categories of perceiving or awareness are as follows:

1. **Physical sensations** (Body Sensing)
   - The five senses—seeing, hearing, feeling/touching, tasting, smelling

- Proprioception of physical sensations
- Tension and relaxation
- Qualities of pain—heat, sharpness, throbbing, stabbing, clenching, and so on
- Balance and acceleration—spinning, movement, vertigo

2. **Energetic sensations** (Subtle Sensing)
   - Proprioception of energetic field/light body
   - Temperature—hot, cold, freezing, burning
   - Expansion and contraction
   - Electromagnetic awareness
   - Attraction and repulsion
   - Vibrations and waves
   - Currents of energy
   - Chakra and/or meridian activations

3. **Feelings/emotions**
   - Feelings—emotional intelligence; the ability to name and skillfully engage emotional experiences
   - Complex emotions—grief, confusion, and so on; emotional experiences made up of many, sometimes conflicting, experiences
   - Extreme emotions—rage, terror, and so on; usually associated with dissociation or cathartic discharges and release

4. **Thoughts/memories/beliefs**
   - Thoughts
   - Memories
   - Beliefs
   - Insights, ideas, and inspirations
   - Perception of time passing

5. **Visions/sounds/symbols/imaginal elements**
   - Images
   - Symbols
   - Shapes

- Frequencies, music, and/or voices
- Colors
- Archetypes
- Animals
- Geometric forms
- Light and darkness
- Memories relived or witnessed

The Five Awareness Practice, detailed on the next page, involves bringing perception and awareness to the five categories listed above. You can use these categories to help name, assess, and navigate your inner journey experience. The more you practice the different ways of perceiving, the more automatic they each become, and you will gradually develop a capacity for experiencing and understanding all these ways of perceiving simultaneously. As mentioned earlier, this is called psychedelic synesthesia. Just like we can hear and see at the same time without thinking, we can also experience a multidimensional immersion of sensation and comprehension with great clarity in psychedelic spaces. Generally speaking, the more we can understand and comprehend an experience, the less anxiety we experience with it. We can then participate longer and explore deeper territories of consciousness with greater resilience, skill, and power.

In a very real way, this is a practice of the inner capacity of understanding and discernment. Before you know what to do with something, you need to know what it is. Also, in a very real way, awareness is by its nature very healing. Using the Five Awareness Practice to simply bring more awareness to a process, and all the ways of perceiving it, is the very act of healing. There's nothing to figure out. Understanding happens as a natural product of awareness.

🫀 The Five Awareness Practice

We begin the practice by getting to know each way of perceiving and sensing one at a time and as well as we can. When under the influence of psychedelics, these senses are heightened and can be overwhelming, so start sober, and when you are intuitively ready incorporate cannabis into your practice, start lightly.

Perform the body scan and explore how much awareness you can bring to each area of yourself. Bring special attention to areas that seem difficult, invisible, or numb. Always remember to breathe, breathe, breathe.

Use the following prompts to help discern your inner experience (you can use the column "other noted outcomes" on the body scan record sheet found in appendix I to keep track your experiences):

1. **Physical sensations**—What are you most aware of in your body? What is calling you? Where is its location? What is its size? If you could trace its shape, what would it be like? Where are the edges of feeling the experience and not feeling it? What is its consistency—soft or hard, tight or loose, rigid, prickly, or smooth? How big is the sensation? How deep in the body does the sensation extend? Is it a solid mass, or does it have threads that extend to other areas?

2. **Energetic sensations**—What energy sensation are you experiencing? Does it have a temperature? Is it still or vibrating? Are the vibrations fast and buzzy or slow like a wave? Do you feel any currents of energy through the space? Unusual sensations of swirling or shifting? Does it feel open and receiving? Is it contracting? What else are you aware of? What do you not notice?

3. **Feelings/emotions**—What emotion are you experiencing when you bring your awareness to this location? Allow yourself to be with it for just a few breaths, fully allowing it to be with you. What else is there? What else is arising? What's underneath that emotion?

4. **Thoughts/memories/beliefs**—Are there any thoughts associated with this experience? Any memories? (Memories can also be very visual, sometimes recalled in a flash, the most extreme being PTSD-type flashbacks that have a strong synesthetic component.) What are you thinking about

the experience? Are you judging it? Accepting it? What beliefs do you have related to it? What are you saying to yourself right now?

5. **Visions/sounds/symbols/imaginal elements**—If the experience were an image, what would it be? What color is it? What does it look like? What is its shape? What other images are there? If it were to tell a story in a statement, what would it say? Are there sounds associated with the image? Music? Listen to the space and see what arises. Does it have a message? What do you not notice? Engage the image; what happens? Go around, through, under, and over the image; what happens?

The Five Awareness Practice and Dross

At the beginning of your practice, you might be most aware of all the different ways dross shows up in your body. It can manifest in the form of tension or pain, a difficult emotion, or even a negative or intrusive thought. The more you remain curious and relax around these sensations, emotions, and thoughts, witness them and work with them using your five inner capacities, the more they are released out of your system.

What happens after that is quite astounding. These difficult sensations begin to manifest in lighter and lighter forms and gifts of understanding, acceptance, empowerment, and transformation. These sensations can be quite positive, and the Five Awareness Practice can be used to cultivate and nourish these sensations, new emotions, and new thoughts. I call this "watering your garden." Let yourself breathe into these positive experiences. Let your body memorize them.

These practices can be difficult at times. It isn't easy to face a traumatic memory or an extreme emotional state. Go at a pace that works for you. What I can say after years of practice and experience is that no matter how difficult it gets, a process always resolves on a positive note and with an incredibly significant gift, in either healing or understanding, or both. This is the "gold in the dark." Stay with the process and keep going.

25

Navigating Strange Terrains and Difficult Experiences

Just as with any powerful psychedelic experience, the psychedelic cannabis experience can be profound, life-transforming, and deeply, deeply evocative. It isn't always easy. In these spaces, we encounter strange terrains, aspects of self we don't want to acknowledge, and a peace and sense of well-being that transcends anything we have ever felt before. Our bodies can dissolve into a pattern of beautiful light. We can move into the darkest areas of our most sacred depths.

Not every experience in a psychedelic state is positive. While psychedelic cannabis is very safe, it's very much like other psychedelics in that we don't take these medicines just to feel better. We have alcohol and opiates for that, and we know how well those are working in the world. We take psychedelics to face a truth, and sometimes it's a hard truth. Sometimes waking up and healing requires us to navigate some pretty difficult spaces. Sometimes to heal trauma, we have to reexperience the memory of it so we can finally release it from our bodies and our psyches.

Adverse reactions to cannabis, even at psychedelic doses, are very uncommon with the right blend, set, and setting. In my experience, a fraction of one percent of psychedelic cannabis users have a strong, negative response to the medicine, and even these are more often a healing and awakening process than any sort of medical emergency. The likelihood of having a difficult experience can be reduced significantly with the right preparation, support, and honest self-assessment. But as much as I wish for you to have a healthy support structure around you, some of us may only have the capacity to start reading a strange little book and exploring the exercises within. If this is your situation, I hope you find some useful guidance in the remaining pages of this chapter. You're not alone, and you're not the first person to experience what you are going through.

When difficult experiences do happen, they're often mild to moderate and generally have a psychosomatic component that can be explored for greater understanding and healing. Mania and psychosis are extremely rare, and the risks can be generally assessed before you even touch the substance. Psychedelic cannabis, when used as outlined in these practices, is very safe, but that doesn't mean you'll always be walking on rainbows and swimming through bliss.

Although cannabis is regularly used to treat nausea, psychedelic cannabis experiences may elicit nausea like other psychedelic medicines do. This nausea generally corresponds to an emotional release of some sort. Vomiting is very rare, but it does happen in our groups on occasion. If you're experiencing nausea, try breathing to the edge of the discomfort and let go. Usually, people stop breathing into their bellies when they start to get nauseous. This may just mean you're moving quickly, and it's okay to slow down a little bit. If you need to vomit, it can be incredibly healing to do so, and it might be quite the experience. You might receive insights as to what you're letting go of, and you're going to feel a lot better afterward. It's safer to have a small trash can with a lining near where you're lying than to try to run to the bathroom. You don't want the big shift from being still to rising quickly and scrambling to the toilet to make you unbalanced or light-headed.

Besides nausea, anxiety is the other most common experience people have on psychedelic cannabis, and it's very normal. Again, if they feel anxiety or panic, most people stop breathing into the belly and start breathing shallowly into the chest or stop breathing altogether, while others might breathe too intensely and quickly, beginning to truly hyperventilate. While cannabis is known to cause anxiety in some people, using the psychedelic cannabis blend makes this less likely, even at higher doses. When it does happen, the remedy is the same—turn your awareness toward your breath. Slow it down and breathe deeply yet gently into the belly. It will be like a wave that will crest, then pass.

Extreme physical discomfort, indicated by frequent body adjustments or a lot of anxiety, may indicate a need to take the CBD antidote to calm the nervous system down a little. Extreme anxiety or panic, while extremely rare, should be immediately addressed so the anxiety doesn't spiral out of control. Remember, you can always pause the experience by adjusting your posture, sitting up, removing your eye covering, and reorienting to the room or having a sip of water. CBD is also a wonderful tool. It isn't somehow a mistake on your part if you choose to use it. Instead, it's healing on your terms and in a way that works for you.

While it isn't easy to do so, it's possible to take too much psychedelic cannabis. Make a note about your dosage and remember the next time you take it to imbibe fewer puffs next time. This is often experienced as an inability to focus or a visual state of very fast-flashing images that seem sometimes a bit random. There may or may not be a theme to it. I like to think of it as my neurons flashing and getting rewired. If this happens, and there's some confusion or an overwhelming question as to what to do, simply let go of trying to do anything at all and return your awareness to your breath. Watch the show and enjoy the ride. Usually, gentle, slow breathing will help you reclaim control and at the very least enjoy the process.

Last but not least is the experience of paranoia, a type of worry not based on fact that elicits a sense of danger and lack of safety in the psychedelic cannabis experience. It isn't uncommon for people who have tried smoking pot and didn't like it, and it's usually elicited by social situations and social anxiety. It can happen in the psychedelic cannabis experience, too, so that's why we put so much effort into building safety into the practice before the session begins.

If you experience paranoia, first try to acknowledge it for what it is. If you're worried about something, ask yourself how likely it is that what you're worried about is going to happen. Sometimes paranoia confuses what's possible with what's probable. It's also a symptom of the cultural trauma we have experienced due to cannabis prohibition. For example, you might get anxious about the possibility of the cops knocking on your door. This is more likely an unresolved trauma than any real possibility of the police dropping by. Pause the experience and look around your space again. Reorient to reality. If you set the space up correctly, you'll be reminded that it's very safe. A history of becoming paranoid from cannabis isn't necessarily a no to trying psychedelic cannabis, but you don't want to minimize the paranoia. Instead, address it. What do you need to help you feel incredibly safe? Even just asking that question itself can be quite healing. This is also why it's so important to only work with people you already know and trust and to make agreements with them regarding safety. This can make a world of difference at the most crucial moments.

When you can acknowledge the paranoia and do a safety check, noting again that you are in fact very safe, turning toward your inner experience of paranoia to examine it becomes possible. It has been my experience that paranoia is a projection of something internal onto something external and is an important, but sometimes scary, process of self-discovery. When we can stay with it like any symptom, it usually passes, and there's important information underneath it. Humans have a profound ability to disown their own process and to put it on something or someone else. In the case of a solo cannabis practice, it might be placed on the medicine, or even the music. Make note of what the content of the paranoia is and see if you can turn your awareness inward. What do you notice about the feeling? Where do you feel it in your body? Breathe with it and relax all around it. These are sometimes the most important moments.

PART FIVE

Breaking the Gate

◆◆◆

As the leadership of the psychedelic movement speaks to mainstreaming psychedelics by keeping them contained in medical and clinical paradigms, on the ground, many, many people are seeking to break free from the mainstream mindsets and lifestyles they realize have been incredibly harmful and unsustainable to them. Many of these people are looking to heal through the use of psychedelics because their mainstream institutions have completely failed them. If you're reading this book, there's a strong possibility you're one of these people, like me.

It's way past time to break open the gate to healing and awakening, and maybe cannabis can do just that. While many psychedelic medicines, including MDMA, have been proposed as primary navigational aids in helping us traverse the wild ocean of possibility, it hasn't yet been possible to implement anything on a large scale. Maybe cannabis can pave the way for that. Most people who want or need MDMA-assisted psychotherapy can't find it, can't access it, can't afford it, or don't qualify for it. Cannabis might be the best tool for us to use in exploring the potential of psychedelics in terms of legal and financial accessibility and safety.

But what skill sets are required to cocreate a psychedelic society that has successfully legalized, regulated, and safely implemented psychedelics for the benefit of its society, not to mention its planet? What if we could start developing those skill sets now, before MDMA and psilocybin are legal? Shouldn't we do so? It isn't at all about tripping. No matter what we're told or what we hear, it just isn't. Psychedelic society is about creating safe environments in which to use these tools in a way that facilitates healing for the benefit of humanity and the planet. Given its qualities, which are outlined in this book, psychedelic cannabis actually has the potential to become one of the best tools we have available. Psychedelic cannabis can not only safely introduce new people to the healing and transformational nature of psychedelic medicines but can also be used as a problem-solving tool for personal and global crises. What if we were to systematically study the potential of this plant? Cannabis for PTSD, cannabis for ecological problem-solving, cannabis for couples therapy and conflict resolution. I believe psychedelic cannabis has the capacity to transform our personal and collective crises by providing us an opportunity to develop a solid resilience to big experiences through the ongoing resolution of trauma and the exploration of transpersonal experiences.

Cannabis needs to be fully recognized as a viable psychedelic medicine as quickly as possible so we can turn toward its study and unlock its true potential for healing and transformation. Because of its safety profile, its legality, and its capacity to scale peak psychedelic experiences in large group settings, cannabis is primed to help large numbers of people heal their own traumas and finally step into who they wish to be, which is paradoxically a deeper expression of who they already are.

I've tried to write down not just what you need to get started with a psychedelic journeywork practice for the intention of healing and waking up, but to be as complete as I can in my message so you can develop these practices in a way that works for you. We're not quite done with that conversation. Let's talk a little more about integration and the context of our lives as the larger setting for these expeditions. There's more than just the experience to break through to true healing, and there are more ways to deepen and expand your practice to impact the crises that face humanity.

26

Stepping into
the Healing Process

There is a saying in alchemy, which you may have heard at some point, that advises, "As above, so below." This message refers to a commonly experienced phenomenon in transformational work, particularly in psychedelic medicine work, where our inner process begins to mirror circumstances in our daily lives, and our daily lives begin to mirror our inner processes. When I heal inside, something outside of me, a life situation, for example, has an opportunity to transform and heal as well. It's common to see the psychedelic healing process of one person actually ripple through entire families and social systems. When one person starts a healing process and starts to wake up to their potential, those around them often begin to wake up as well and become part of the overall healing process. This is the holotropic process of the universe that we're a part of naturally unfolding. Everything will move toward wholeness if we let it. And if we let one thing move toward wholeness, it ripples through other things, other situations, in a cascading butterfly effect.

Integrating the psychedelic experience into everyday life is a stepping-into process. There is no way to fulfill the psychedelic vision in one simple decision, one big leap. It just doesn't work that way. What you're experiencing is real healing, but it takes time, repeated decision-making, and actions toward health to anchor those changes in your body and mind. Equally, what you're seeing in these experiences is the holistic vision of an idea, the completion of a big process, not the next step. It is there to inspire you to do the hard work required to realize that vision. Nothing more. What does it look like to create an ongoing practice that continuously engages this hard work? What if the vision isn't at all important? What if what's most important is the actual process? What if we could orient toward an ongoing process of healing and find relief and inspiration in that healing instead of waiting to be fully healed before we choose to step out of suffering?

THE MEDICINE PATH

I'd like to use the analogy of a snake moving to add some context to this discussion. A snake moves its body from left to right in an oscillating motion that moves the snake forward. Another analogy might be a paddle at the back of a boat moving back and forth to propel the boat forward. The point is, if you only push in one direction, you'll go in circles. A sustainable path using psychedelic medicines involves equal parts inner journeywork experiences and external, real-life experiences and actions. If one is missing, real progress forward isn't possible.

What would it look like to move like a snake or be paddled like a boat and to skillfully navigate a space that incorporated both the psychedelic cannabis practices and the real-world work of trying to implement the ideas, solutions, and creative visions offered to you in your internal state? As above, so below. We test the validity of our inner experience by seeing how it impacts our real-world experience. Keep your eye on your intention—that's your direction—but allow yourself to fluidly move through the possibilities that lead to it. Very rarely is the path a direct one. This process is more like exploring a large garden on a beautiful day, with some adventures thrown in here and there to keep you interested. There is more than one path to the outcome you desire, and some paths are easier than others.

TRANSPERSONAL SPACES

The fact is, we're not doing this work in an isolation chamber. We are part of an ecosystem of overlapping dynamics that may or may not always be in our best interest. Some of these dynamics we have agency over, and some are bigger than us and might only be influenced through sustained, collective effort. The journey toward the legalization of cannabis is a great example. There are competing interests, allies (but also adversaries), obstacles, and even external forms of energetic dross.

Psychedelic cannabis, as well as the other psychedelics, gives us the experience of working with and confronting internal oppositions to healing and waking up. In a very real sense, the "as above, so below" model is alive and well in this dynamic because the skill sets and resiliencies developed for internal work are the exact same ones we use to navigate and successfully engage this wild and crazy world we live in. These skill sets are the five inner capacities we're working to develop that allow us to build an exceptionally sturdy ship to navigate the treacherous waters ahead. The successful development of these ships, both individually and collectively, will determine how successful we are in navigating the global crises ahead.

Be mindful that difficult processes don't necessarily mean you're headed in the wrong direction. These may manifest in the form of a difficult emotional process, a healing crisis, a big event at work, or in a relationship. Remember that a symptom is something halfway out. What if we can work with external situations just as we do internal explorations? What if we can use the same tools to heal, transform, and cocreate our shared, collective experience? These crises may just be what healing looks like; just as painful contractions are part of a natural birthing process.

Remember to chop some wood, carry water, and know that real transformation often occurs and is held sustainably after deliberate effort. People didn't just intend to go to the moon and back; they built a rocket first.

27

A Community
Experiment in Healing

Medicinal Mindfulness is a community of psychedelic healers and explor-
ers. It is through the spirit of community and sharing that we present
these ideas to our larger, global community to do our part in helping all
of us transform our pain and our struggles together. While we envision a
society where we can come together in beautiful *heartships* (see p. 193) to
engage in these practices, as a community, I've come to realize we're still
many years away from these possibilities on any sort of large scale. The
intention of this book is to hopefully catalyze this process by inviting
those who are interested into a vision of what's actually possible.

Our local Medicinal Mindfulness community is fortunate to live
in a city where ongoing group psychedelic cannabis experiences can be
facilitated openly. We're also more than blessed that we actually have
a community gathering place to facilitate these group experiences. An
incredibly unlikely combination of events and circumstances came
together to make this work happen: Colorado became one of the first
states to legalize cannabis, my own unusual professional path helped
me gain the skill sets, experience, and theoretical understanding to
implement psychedelic programs with cannabis, and a community
space became available that was big enough to allow us to practice and
develop these experiences. I didn't know it at the time, but it turned out
we were working in the only location, in the only city, and in the only

state in the country that would allow us to do this work openly. I didn't know how special it was when we started, so many thanks to my brothers and sisters in the work who made all this possible.

The wonderful private yoga studio and community gathering place in which we work has allowed us to think really big. It was this space, in which we could cram just twenty-nine people, that taught us it was possible to facilitate large, incredibly meaningful psychedelic groups in a way that was completely safe. It also inspired us to design heart-ships, which are buildings for large intentional community gatherings that incorporate psychedelic cannabis experiences with live music in a container of safety and support. We envision these heartships indoors as well as outdoors in an open-air space. The heartship designs shown in the figure below are for twenty-five-, fifty-, and one hundred-person psychedelic experiences.

What would it take to share these experiences with as many people as possible? What institutional framework is required? Given the potential of this medicine, what do we focus on? What does the world most need in this moment?

My answer is this: as a global community, we desperately need transformational healing opportunities that use psychedelics in a safe and supportive community and on a very large scale. It isn't that these practices are necessarily spiritual; it's that the spiritual aspects of these experiences are a natural by-product of the transformational states they elicit. The community that gathers for these events, along with the new friendships made among its members, sometimes provides the most meaning to those who experience it.

In those moments, as we look around to see that others are holding pipes containing cannabis, others inspired by this work who have also had deeply healing and deeply meaningful experiences, we begin to finally realize we're not alone or crazy or unhealthy in our profound curiosity of the states that the psychedelic medicines elicit. Psychedelic cannabis made all of this possible.

Cannabis is truly the first psychedelic that broke the gate that blocks

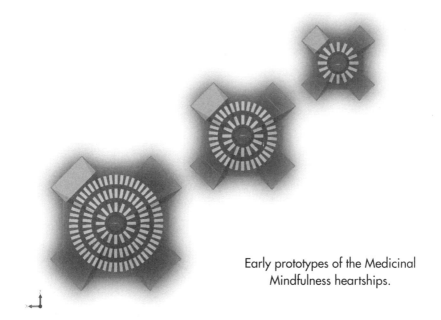

Early prototypes of the Medicinal
Mindfulness heartships.

us from our own healing and from stepping into our full potential, not just as individuals, but as entire societies. This is a huge vision, and it has taken me years to trust it's actually possible and something worth working for, rather than a grandiose, delusional dream. This is something we're already actively doing right now. I work full-time as a Cannabis-Assisted Psychedelic Therapist. I've trained hundreds of people, and communities are forming in several cities already in the United States and Canada. No research proposals have to be approved by institutional review boards. We don't have to convince the government to stop growing shitty weed so we can do research with these practices. We just have to consider the possibilities outside the norm, outside of what we've been told. And the thing is, in a lot of places, these medicines aren't even illegal, just underutilized.

I wish this type of community for you, but I suspect that I may not be the one who will create it. You'll be that person. What does it look like to live into this potential? I think it's just a simple stepping into process, as outlined in the previous chapter. That's how I did it. I asked myself over and over again, what's my intention, what's the image of that intention made manifest, and what's the next step I can take to achieve it? I started by working on myself, then my friends and family, then groups and clients.

What would it look like if that were replicated on a large scale?

Trying to implement a big idea too quickly or while skipping necessary steps is one of the most common mistakes psychedelic medicine people make during integration. It can be too much too quickly, and it can overwhelm our nervous system and our capacity to engage the work proactively. As you play with the stepping-into model, made possible by cannabis, ask yourself what you're ready to explore in your life at this moment. Don't jump into the big picture yet. It really is alright to devote your full attention to healing yourself. You matter. Being of service can come later, if that's what you wish to do. If you're in a place where it isn't safe to practice openly, practice by yourself and start gaining the skills and experience that will help you support others. You'll know when you're ready to take the next step because you'll feel it inside your own body.

We would like to invite you into a social experiment, as well. As you work on your solo practice, just getting started in exploring these big spaces, you're going to have a lot of questions about the work that a book like this can't directly answer. There's a lot of time spent figuring things out. That said, we're creating an online structure to bring the psychedelic cannabis community together into shared, solo practices within a container of safety and support. Please visit our program website for more information. To help get you started, I've made available a free, guided body scan meditation you can download to add to your music sets. It's available under the Media tab of the Medicinal Mindfulness website. A guided meditation series is currently being developed that can help guide a solo practitioner through the entire psychedelic cannabis experience.

Can we trust the guidance of the psychedelic cannabis experience and intuition and *live into* new possibilities? For me, the answer is a simple and obvious yes.

Again, if you use these practices to heal yourself, to find relief, to turn toward achieving what you really care about in this world, that's enough. As someone who's had to do the work himself, I recognize how difficult it can be and how much time it takes to step into real healing, real transformation. That said, you might find that as you develop your practice,

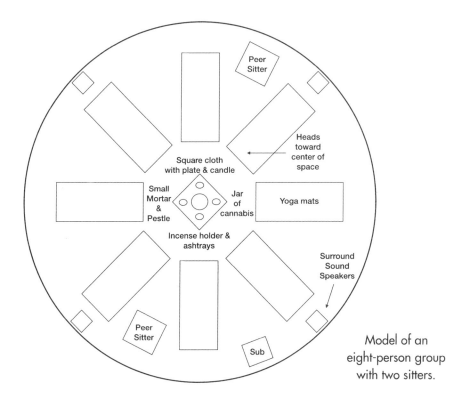

Model of an
eight-person group
with two sitters.

you have opportunities and desires to share this work with others. You might see a need in your family, or friends, or community. And while some might not be open to this work, others will be. It isn't unrealistic to consider small groups will begin to independently organize to safely share these experiences.

When the right conditions are met, all of which have been outlined in this book, there's virtually no reason you can't start creating a small gathering experience of your own with your friends. If the meditations aren't yet psychedelic, if they're *just* breathwork, they're a big step toward shared psychedelic experiences and are still very healing. Again, the community that gathers is the most important factor here. We are the medicine we've been looking for.

Maybe your music wasn't quite right, or maybe the medicine could have been stronger. Maybe you didn't have visions. That's more than okay. I know this because I do this work all the time and know it is possible if you don't give up. Learn from the experience, adjust it as needed, and keep going. Healing still happens even if it isn't psychedelic.

Start practicing in your living room. When you're ready, start sharing it with people you know and love. Start asking whether any of the yoga studios, dispensaries, gathering spaces, churches, and temples you think might be interested would be open to these practices (you can always require clean-smelling vaporizers over pipes). If you present yourself as professionally as possible when you reach out to community gathering spaces, someone will eventually say yes to this. That's what happened with us. The laws and societal views are so rapidly changing that within a few years, there will hundreds of locations open to these ideas, and some will be in your area. Along the entire West Coast of the United States, and throughout Canada, it's already legal to do these practices. Social-use gathering places have just come into law in Colorado, as well. Because of the work we've already done, it'll be a simple next step for us to facilitate large group experiences. We'll already have a community trained for it.

PSYCHEDELIC SITTERS SCHOOL

Facilitating psychedelic experiences is a genuine occupation akin to becoming a professional practitioner in other healing modalities. There's a lot of overlap in these skill sets with therapists, ministers, massage therapists, and other healers, but we don't necessarily have to be a professional healer to safely facilitate psychedelic experiences. This is also true for psychedelic cannabis. At some point, you may be ethically required to develop your practice in a way that conforms with certain professional guidelines through training and education. While this book is in part written to convince professionals to consider the concept of psychedelic cannabis, it's primarily written for those who are ready to step into these practices in their personal lives. This is fundamentally a book about psychedelic harm reduction.

Hanging out with your friends and experimenting is one thing. Working professionally is something else. I know this because I've made it through some mistakes and not-quite-right experiments, and each stage has led to new opportunities to screw it up all over again. I give thanks every day for just making it this far in this wild jungle. So if I've cut a path through the thick underbrush of consciousness, I don't want you to necessarily cut a path parallel to mine. I would much rather you start from the place I've made it to by using these practices and ideas and then go in a direction you're curious to explore. What do these practices look like when used in conjunction with X therapeutic or healing or creative modality? Where else can we take it?

At some point, you might begin to wonder how your experiences objectively compare to established practices. How does your blend compare to ours? How deep is your practice really diving compared to other people's experiences? What is its true potential? Medicinal Mindfulness hosts regular local community events in Boulder, Colorado, and you're invited to check them out at any time. To get a deep-dive education, we have created an online and in-person training program called Psychedelic Sitters School. You can also come to Boulder for a private retreat.

Are you looking to step into a healing practice with psychedelics as a professional? The Psychedelic Sitters School was the first psychedelic therapy training program to accept people from professional backgrounds other than clinicians and medical practitioners. We sincerely believe you don't have to be a trained therapist or a medical professional to be a skillful and ethical psychedelic guide. The program offers everything required to step into this work safely. We'll show you how to do the work, facilitate the experience with others, and provide substantive conversations regarding legality and the ethical requirements to bring psychedelic cannabis into a professional practice. Or you can just come and plan on having a wonderful transformational experience.

As Cannabis-Assisted Psychedelic Therapy was further developed I realized it was part of a more inclusive modality we call Mindfulness-Based Psychedelic Therapy. To learn more about these programs and psychedelic therapy modalities, please visit our Psychedelic Sitters School website or turn to appendix 2 of this book.

We're actively speaking to these ideas because it's possible that an entire field associated with psychedelic cannabis can be created. If you have a particular profession, don't quit your day job. Use it instead to support the development of psychedelic communities. Our community comprises professionals and students from all walks of life. We need accountants, marketing experts, architects, farmers, teachers, computer programmers, everyone. All hands on deck.

Work for social justice and ecological causes. The world needs you. If you find a crack in the establishment that a psychedelic-inspired idea can fit into, pursue it and grow into it. For those who are ready, start introducing the work to leaders in your already established communities. Wherever there's an opening, take the chance and step into it. You don't have to jump into the unknown, the scary darkness, or take radical risks to be an ally to others. What does it look like to take that next step?

28

The Slower We Go,
the Faster We Get There ...
and We're Running Out of Time

When I first completed the self-published version of this book a couple of years ago, it happened to be April 20, 2019, the seventh anniversary of our program. In the beginning, now nearly a decade ago, the concept of psychedelic cannabis wasn't even in my field of awareness, let alone something I would end up devoting my life to. That happened just a few years later, though, when cannabis became legal here. A lot has changed since then.

It's such an unusual thing to consider that April 20, or 4/20, the international holiday for cannabis, happened to be the day we finally legally registered the counseling company that was to become the Center for Medicinal Mindfulness. And here it is again, on the day I write the last page of the final draft of this book on cannabis. It's hard not to place some meaning on that.

It's just pot, right? I was so wrong. I look back at those early moments and realize I saw all of these possibilities, even then, but they seemed so far out of reach. I've gained a wealth of experience, actually knowing what it's like to be continually surrounded by miraculous moments of transformation and healing. I know, beyond a doubt, how powerful this work is. It's an embodied, felt sense. I feel it in my bones. So what does the next chapter look like? Where do we take this from here?

It is now obvious that this next cycle will be one of ongoing crisis, climate or otherwise, from the local to the international level. We're already in the throes of it. I consider myself to be decently awake, but it was only a few months ago that I started to fully comprehend the dire nature of our present predicament. We may have no more than a decade to change our entire society so we can avoid and subvert global ecological disaster. Ten. More. Years.

I wasn't quite ready to write this book, but what I want doesn't really matter in this context. Crisis signifies an event of both great danger and incredible opportunity. We can get hurt, and this sharpens our senses, and in that sharpness we see new possibilities for skillful action. I've seen this firsthand. There is something about a crisis that makes us much more honest with ourselves. The skill sets and resiliencies that are developed through the resolution of trauma are particularly useful in these honest moments and may be what make us the most adept at engaging the challenges ahead.

As much as I'd like to implement cannabis-assisted therapy modalities the supposed "right way," through research and academics, we just might not have time to solely focus on these paths. We need healing now. I can think of no better way for each of us, individually, to heal our trauma, than working with psychedelic cannabis. Imagine the collective difference that this could make in working through these challenging times. These practices, and other medicine-related practices, may create the tipping point that we so desperately need right now to finally transform our society toward real sustainability and justice. Is everything in this book correct? I don't know, but what I do know is that these skill sets are useful for their purpose. And they're especially useful in the situation we're in.

We are all tasked with solving the largest dilemma we've ever been confronted with: to participate in the evolution of our species or face global collapse. And somehow, each of our own healing and awakening processes is a primary, core, vital factor in our overall success as a species. There's no way I could have made it this far on this journey exploring the potential of psychedelic cannabis without healing myself along the way. Healing myself was a necessary part of the discovery process.

And it's true: the gentler we are, the slower we go, the more permission we have to take care of ourselves, the faster we actually move through these transformational processes. Personally, this healing has required me to go so slowly, so gently, that I seemed to be nearly standing still at times, silently witnessing. Yet, at the same time, I've had to acknowledge and let myself fully feel another, equally important core truth that has caused me significant anxiety and fear: while healing requires gentleness, stillness, and slowing down, we're simply running out of time to do this work. Both understandings are necessary.

All hands on deck. Practice the crafts you know. The wild ocean is calling, and we're being pulled out of our safe harbors by forces beyond our control. Use what you know, and if you're inspired, call in cannabis as an ally for your own adventure into the unknown.

Above all else, I wish you safe travels. Wherever you go.

APPENDIX 1

Body Scan Record Sheet

After completing a body scan as part of your mindfulness journey, use the table on the next page to record your observations over time. Use your observations to help you notice patterns that may lead to breakthroughs in your healing.

The "active" period refers to the actual body scan practice of moving your awareness through the body locations. The "passive" period refers to a period of rest after the active scanning period.

Medicinal Mindfulness Body Scan Record Sheet

Date	Time of Day	Duration		Adjectives to Describe Experience	Other Noted Outcomes
		Active	Passive		

APPENDIX 2

Additional Resources

MEDICINAL MINDFULNESS COURSES AND EVENTS

We at the Center for Medicinal Mindfulness recognize you might have questions about your practice, and we want to provide as much support to you as possible. If you are seeking additional training, we have a wealth of courses available. Listed below are some of our primary training programs and events.

Core Training Program

Level 1: Foundations in Mindfulness-Based Psychedelic Therapy— Facilitation logistics and mindfulness-based sitting practices for curating professional-level psychedelic cannabis experiences

Level 2: Psychedelic Guide Training—Additional guide skill sets that allow practitioners to deepen psychedelic cannabis experiences for their clients

Level 3: Advanced Practices in Mindfulness-Based Psychedelic Therapy—Using psychedelic cannabis to address clinical concerns such as PTSD and other mental health issues that require additional therapeutic support to safely navigate

Additional Programs

Psychedelic First Aid/CPR Certification—Wilderness first aid training, CPR certification, and mental health crisis intervention and assessments

DMTx Psychonaut Training—Advanced psychonaut training in preparation for Extended-State DMT expeditions

Additional Courses—Transpersonal Theory and Practice, Psychedelic Ethics & Multicultural Competency, and EcoPsychedelics (visit the Psychedelic Sitters School website for more information)

Annual Community Events

Wellness Retreat & Community Gathering: An Expedition in Psychedelic Cannabis—An annual, five-day international community gathering in Colorado on a five-hundred-acre ranch to play, rejuvenate, and journey with psychedelic cannabis in a wonderful community context

DMTx retreats—Extended-State DMT retreats are for experienced psychonauts and experts in transformational fields, such as climate scientists, computer programmers, artists, and social activists (visit the DMTx website for more information.)

Visit our Medicinal Mindfulness and Psychedelic Sitters School websites for additional resources and to join our community of psychedelic travelers. Additional handouts and resources available through our training program include the following:

- Psychedelic Experience Agreement
- Guidelines for Testing the Authenticity of Intuition
- Integration Sheet
- Preparation Sheet
- Journey Notes Sheet

- Music set playlists
- Online community forum
- Free body scan guided meditation and access to additional guided meditations

ADDITIONAL MEDICINAL MINDFULNESS ONLINE RESOURCES

Our program and website are always evolving. You can also use our website to download PDFs and explore links to music and other resources, most notably the *Medicinal Mindfulness Psychedelic Integration Guidebook* written by Medicinal Mindfulness cofounder, Alison McQueen, MA, LPC, ATR, and designed to help guide you through your integration process.

The guided meditations found under the media tab are as follows:

- **Guided Body Scan**—25-minute guided body scan meditation. Good for ongoing practice and adding to the beginning of a long and gentle healing session.
- **Guided Body Scan with Additional Meditation Music**—Same meditation with 35 more minutes of gentle music (60 minutes total). Great for ongoing practice, self-care, and sleep aid.
- **Short Body Scan**—15-minute guided body scan. Good for adding to the beginning of a solo cannabis session when you want to have more time for the music set.
- **Five Awareness Practice**—11-minute practice of tracking with the five awareness practice used in conjunction with the music playlist beside it by playing both at the same time on the computer. Again, there are also apps that pair meditations with different music.

THE MEDICINAL MINDFULNESS
SAFE COMMUNITY POLICY

To support the development of important safety standards for the use of psychedelic medicines in spiritual, clinical, and community use settings, and to have an ongoing dialogue about medicine use that is safe from harassment and abuse, Medicinal Mindfulness has developed the Medicinal Mindfulness Safe Community Policy as a community code of conduct. More information can be found on our website under the About tab.

MENTAL HEALTH AND
PSYCHEDELIC HEALTH RESOURCES

As a mental health and psychedelic harm reduction and education program, the Center for Medicinal Mindfulness encourages our readers who are struggling to reach out to someone for help. You are not alone. There are many national programs that offer specialized mental health services.

American Pregnancy Helpline: 866-942-6466
Childhelp National Child Abuse Hotline: 800-4-A-Child
    (800-422-4453)
Comprehensive Resources Helpline Center: Dial 211
Depression and Bipolar Support Alliance: 800-826-3632
Grief Recovery Institute: 818-907-9600
LGBT National Hotline: 888-843-4564
Mental Health America: 800-969-6MHA (6642)
National Alliance on Mental Illness: 800-950-NAMI (6264)
National Council on Alcoholism and Drug Dependence: 800-622-2255
National Domestic Violence Hotline: 800-799-7233
National Drug Helpline: 888-633-3239
National Human Trafficking Hotline: 888-373-7888

National Network for Immigrant and Refugee Rights: 510-465-1984

National Nurses On-Call Hotline: 816-276-6405

National Poison Control: 800-222-1222

National Sexual Assault Hotline: 800-656-HOPE (4673)

National Suicide Prevention Hotline: 800-273-8255

Planned Parenthood National Hotline: 800-230-7526

Psychedelic Integration Support Resources

Center for Medicinal Mindfulness: Psychedelic therapy, psychotherapy, Psychedelic Sitters School, breathwork and cannabis events

TripSit Chat website: Guidance and support with regard to harm reduction when using drugs

Multidisciplinary Association for Psychedelic Studies (MAPS): See the integration therapist directory on their website

Psychedelic Support Network website: Client-centered care from trusted, nonjudgmental health professionals

Spiritual Emergence Network USA website: Support service and referral to licensed or trained local mental health care professionals for individuals that are experiencing psychospiritual difficulties

About Daniel McQueen and the Center for Medicinal Mindfulness

Daniel McQueen is the executive director of the Center for Medicinal Mindfulness and is a professional psychedelic specialist. He has a master's degree in transpersonal counseling psychology from Naropa University and over twenty years of experience exploring psychedelic medicines. In 2012, he cofounded the Center for Medicinal Mindfulness with his wife, Alison McQueen, MA, LPC, ATR, as a psychedelic harm-reduction program in Boulder, Colorado, which has since evolved into an international psychedelic therapy training program focusing on Mindfulness-Based Psychedelic Therapy, Cannabis-Assisted Psychedelic Therapy, and Cannabis-Assisted Psychotherapy.

When cannabis became legal in Colorado in 2014, Daniel began facilitating group psychedelic experiences using special blends of cannabis that induce psychedelic states and mimic the combined effects of MDMA, psilocybin, ayahuasca, and DMT. These events, called Conscious Cannabis Circles, helped develop the potential for cannabis to become a useful psychedelic within a somatically oriented, mindfulness-based, transpersonally aligned, and clinically informed protocol to treat trauma, PTSD, and other significant psychological concerns. In addition to his work in private practice facilitating individual psychedelic experiences with cannabis, Daniel facilitates training retreats and online courses for the Psychedelic Sitters School Psychedelic Therapy Training Program.

Other programs the Center for Medicinal Mindfulness has developed include the Psychedelic Shine speaker series and community gatherings, a monthly Community Breathwork program, and the Extended-State DMT Program, also known as DMTx. The DMTx program explores the extreme growth edge of the psychedelic movement.

Under the leadership of Alison McQueen, MA, LPC, ATR, clinical director of Medicinal Mindfulness and sub-investigator of the MAPS MDMA-assisted psychotherapy for PTSD Phase 2 trials, Medicinal Mindfulness has organized a clinical and medical team that facilitates cannabis-assisted psychotherapy and ketamine-assisted psychotherapy for the treatment of PTSD and other clinical disorders, alongside art therapy, trauma resolution therapy, and transpersonal and mindfulness-based psychotherapy. The clinic provides psychedelic crisis support, addictions counseling, integration support, nutrition support, and psychedelic harm-reduction education.

Daniel lives with his family in Boulder, Colorado, and is a proud father, a writer, and a psychedelic community organizer.

Index